GOOD BETTER BEST

Wines

A No-Nonsense Guide to Popular Wines

GOOD BETTER BEST

Wines

A No-Nonsense Guide to Popular Wines

Carolyn Evans Hammond

ALPHA

A member of Penguin Group (USA) Inc.

ALPHA BOOKS

Published by the Penguin Group

Penguin Group (USA) Inc., 375 Hudson Street, New York, New York 10014, USA

Penguin Group (Canada), 90 Eglinton Avenue East, Suite 700, Toronto, Ontario M4P 2Y3, Canada (a division of Pearson Penguin Canada Inc.)

Penguin Books Ltd., 80 Strand, London WC2R 0RL, England

Penguin Ireland, 25 St. Stephen's Green, Dublin 2, Ireland (a division of Penguin Books Ltd.)

Penguin Group (Australia), 250 Camberwell Road, Camberwell, Victoria 3124, Australia (a division of Pearson Australia Group Pty. Ltd.)

Penguin Books India Pvt. Ltd., 11 Community Centre, Panchsheel Park, New Delhi—110 017, India

Penguin Group (NZ), 67 Apollo Drive, Rosedale, North Shore, Auckland 1311, New Zealand (a division of Pearson New Zealand Ltd.)

Penguin Books (South Africa) (Pty.) Ltd., 24 Sturdee Avenue, Rosebank, Johannesburg 2196, South Africa

Penguin Books Ltd., Registered Offices: 80 Strand, London WC2R 0RL, England

International Standard Book Number: 978-1-59257-977-8
Library of Congress Catalog Card Number: 2009909618

12   8

Interpretation of the printing code: The rightmost number of the first series of numbers is the year of the book's printing; the rightmost number of the second series of numbers is the number of the book's printing. For example, a printing code of 10-1 shows that the first printing occurred in 2010.

Printed in the United States of America

Note: This publication contains the opinions and ideas of its author. It is intended to provide helpful and informative material on the subject matter covered. It is sold with the understanding that the author and publisher are not engaged in rendering professional services in the book. If the reader requires personal assistance or advice, a competent professional should be consulted.

The author and publisher specifically disclaim any responsibility for any liability, loss, or risk, personal or otherwise, which is incurred as a consequence, directly or indirectly, of the use and application of any of the contents of this book.

Trademarks: All terms mentioned in this book that are known to be or are suspected of being trademarks or service marks have been appropriately capitalized. Alpha Books and Penguin Group (USA) Inc. cannot attest to the accuracy of this information. Use of a term in this book should not be regarded as affecting the validity of any trademark or service mark.

Most Alpha books are available at special quantity discounts for bulk purchases for sales promotions, premiums, fund-raising, or educational use. Special books, or book excerpts, can also be created to fit specific needs.

For details, write: Special Markets, Alpha Books, 375 Hudson Street, New York, NY 10014.

For Geoffrey.

Contents

Introduction

If anyone can wobble into verbose, irrelevant, wayward, noun-strewn-as-adjective criticism, it's a wine writer. I know. It's my profession. But who cares if the grapes were handpicked by Jean-Paul with the blue beret and his three sons, then thrice sorted, pneumatically pressed, fermented with wild yeasts, aged in large old oak barrels, and blended with 2.4 percent Semillon to enhance the mouthfeel? Or that the vines grew in soil rich in calcareous Kimmeridgian clay and Jean-Paul's wife Martine once drank the 1967 vintage with Pierre Bardot, the fifth cousin of Bridget Bardot?

What does the wine taste like? Is it a good price? And is it available at the wine shop or supermarket down the street? That's what matters, especially when you're looking for a great-tasting, five- or ten-buck bottle to enjoy midweek.

Sure, a little story is interesting conversation lube, but talk of wine can quickly dwindle into mind-parchingly dry drivel about vineyard location, vintage quality, and the tepid tedium of winemaking techniques like malolactic fermentation, micro-oxygenation, and filtration.

With this book, I'm putting my foot down. Slamming my fist on the table and giving you the stuff that matters. The dirt. The goods. The short, sweet, critical information on what the wine tastes like so you can get on with drinking. I sample, you drink. Deal?

With that in mind, I've tasted the top brands in the United States. These are the brands you know, the bottles you recognize, and the names you trust to make wines that suit you and everyone you know.

And I'm not pulling these brands from thin air. Each year a respected market research company called The Beverage Information Group publishes the *Wine Handbook*, which includes a ranking of the top 120 wine brands based on volumes sold across the United States. I've based this book on those brands. Additionally, a few marketing and public relations people persuaded me to include names outside the top 120 by nearly breaking into arias about the greatness of certain bottles, then anchoring their hand-waving enthusiasm with compelling information to show the wines are both popular and widely available. So I tasted these bottles, too, on your behalf.

Just how popular are the brands in this book? The top brand sold the equivalent of 270 million regular-size bottles in 2007, and most brands represented here sold no fewer than 4.8 million bottles in the same 12-month period. These aren't wines people buy and go, *meh*, and don't buy again. They're repeat purchases. The numbers bear that out. Plus, the wines are not just stocked at a handful of out-of-the-way wine boutiques; they're the most widely available bottles in the United States.

So what I've done with this guide is compare grapes to grapes. All the $5 to $7.99 Chardonnays were tasted side by side to determine which ones are best, as were the $8 to $10.99s, and the $11 to $15 offerings. For this book, $15 is the cutoff because volumes drop considerably beyond that price. Wines over $15 are generally made in smaller amounts, aren't as widely stocked, and so aren't relevant to these pages. The only exception to the $15 cut-off is Chapter 19 on dessert wine, which includes bottles up to $30.

What I've done with this book is represent the most popular varieties sold in the United States—the Chardonnays, Pinot Grigios, Sauvignon Blancs, Merlots, Cabernet

Sauvignons, and so forth—with a chapter devoted to each. To cover some other interesting stuff, a couple of catchall chapters were thrown in, titled "Other Great Whites" and "Other Great Reds." And to account for the usually terrible but sometimes quite drinkable wine that costs less than $5 per bottle—or the equivalent value in boxed form—I've tacked on a chapter called, "Good Deals at Super-Low Prices."

I might add that Americans drink more domestic wine than imported, so the regional cross-section of wines here follows suit. A bit of Argentinean, Australian, Chilean, French, German, Italian, New Zealand, Portuguese, South African, and Spanish wine is included, but there's a whole lot of great-value American stuff.

This book not only recommends the good, better, and best wines in every important category with bottle images to help you find them in the shops, it also slips in other interesting bits of information including food pairing suggestions, best serving temperatures, and factoids for conversation fodder—such as the names of the best-selling Pinot Grigios in America.

A useful guide to popular wines is necessary given that Americans already spend more money on wine than any other nation. The United States will drink more wine than any other country by 2012, and the vast majority of the wine Americans drink is popular big brands that sell for less than $15 per bottle. It makes sense; although thousands of wines exist, big brands like Barefoot, Beringer, Cavit, Korbel, and Rosemount deliver great value for the money. They taste the same year to year, they're widely available, and they sport clear and recognizable labels. And of course they're made to appeal to the many rather than the few, so you can count on them not to let you down.

While wine snobs with raised pinkies are buying, swirling, and sniffing the wines that cost two arms and a leg per bottle and are tediously hard to find, the rest of America is just drinking wine. Popular wine. Big-brand wine. Ironically, a disproportionate amount of wine writing focuses on big-ticket, small-scale wines in infinite detail, yet no book has ever focused on ranking popular big brands—until now.

One reason little ink has been spilled on big brands is that there's a stigma attached to them. Among wine critics and connoisseurs, they're often seen as less interesting. Too commercial. Too generic. Too industrial—as if quantity has an inverse relationship with quality, which of course it doesn't. Uninspiring wines are made by both big and small producers, but still this stigma persists.

Among some wine critics, it's even believed that big brands are simply a means for driving shareholder value, leading to marketing that overpromises and bottles that underdeliver. Though this is the case sometimes, it's certainly not always true. It makes better business sense to do the opposite: use economies of scale to make wines that overperform at each price point and then fan awareness with honest marketing.

Sure, big brands use economies of scale to muscle into the market, and it tugs at the heart to watch cold, hard market forces squeeze out smaller winemakers. With little money to toss toward marketing, merchandising, and advertising and without the quantities of wine or dollars needed to secure wide distribution, the little guy loses and the big guy wins—simple as that. It's especially difficult for wine critics to watch this happen when we spend much time visiting smaller winemakers, seeing the dirt under their fingernails, feeling the grip of passion behind their words, and appreciating their daily struggle with those gnarled vines to produce wines of beauty, place, and often pedigree. On some level, it's hard not to fall in love with these producers when they charm you with their honest lifestyle, take you into their homes, make you food, and court you with their most treasured wines. But the people behind the big brands work hard, too, and their wines couldn't be successful without consumer consent—without making wine that people like to drink, can find on the shelves, and count on for pleasure. Big brands are there to turn to as reliable, go-to wines for Wednesday's pasta, Friday's hamburgers, or that upcoming wedding reception for 100 of your closest friends and family.

The trouble is, with upward of 20 big-brand eight-buck Chardonnays on the shelf side by side, it's hard to know which one to choose. You certainly can't taste or even smell them all before you buy, and there aren't many scratch-and-sniff labels. So clearly it's high time some critic took a good, hard look—and taste—of the most popular wines in the United States, squirreled out the best in each style and price category, and independently published the results. Therein lies the purpose of this book. I hope you find it useful.

Acknowledgments

There are many people to thank for their help with this book. A lot of people have gone out of their way to provide samples, images, thoughts, and information, including Maria Allan, Isabel Alvarez Bulacio, Jo Andrews, Gian Alfonso Negretti, Kurt Arens, Gustavo Arroyat, Joseph Arthur Cammarata, Giuseppe Barraco, Mary Beltsidis, Eva Bertran, Giancarlo Bianchetti, Robert Bower, Martha Champaigne, David Churchill, Kelly Conrad,

Beppi Crosariol, Alison Davies, Craig De Blois, Mark Donaldson, Krista Drew, Harry Drung, Rachel DuBois, Pierre Dumas, Wanda Erickson, Holly Evans, Jim Ferguson, Iris Fessler, Chris Fleming, Mark Fogleman, Juliana French-Arnold, Odilia Galar-Noel, Massimiliano Giacomini, Emily Gorton, Pamela Graviet, Bill Haddleton, Russell Hammond, Dana Lee Harris, Toni Harron, Margie Healy, Michael Heintz, Susan Hensley, Rebecca Hopkins, Elizabeth Hooker, Gladys Horiuchi, Jenna Hudson, Nicole Hughes, Nick Ising, Kendall Johnson, Kelley Jones, Laurie Jones, Howard Kaman, Jillian Kasbergen, Sabrina Keraudren, Jane Kettlewell, Christopher Klau, Jim Knapp, Lily Lane, Peter Lang, Robert Larsen, Katy Leese, Mari Lou Lenon, Jim Lindsay, Keith Love, Wah-Ching Luk, Angela Lyons, Andrew MacDonald, Vanessa Manzione, Isabelle McDonnell, Mark McFadyen, Josephine Meessen, Sheridan Merriex, Tammy Mikus, Ally Miller, Liz Morellato, Susan Muniak, Pam Novak, Stacey Nunes, Libby Nutt, Roberto Occoffer, Erica Odden, Silvina Palacio, Heather Parker, Nancy Paasch, Cindy Paup, Maggie Peak, Jim Pearson, Michael Peck, Alberto Pecora, Giovanni Pecora, Claudia Pehar, Melanie Pyne, Kathy Pyrce, Mike Rich, Elizabeth Robertis, Javier Rodriguez, Caroline Roy, Hillary Ruesch, Shilah Salmon, Russell Sandham, Laurie Schaefer, Bethany Scherline, Patricia Schneider, Ashleigh Sconce, Caroline Shaw, Peter Sheehan, Lizzy Silva, Maria Soledad Rodriguez, Roberta Speronello, Colleen Stewart, Alison Stigers, Tom Stowell, Loree Stroup, Anne Theunissen, Deborah Thomas, Kim Tomlinson, Barbara Travaglia, Becky Vuolo-Paglia, Caitlin Wellman, Friday Werner, Jenny Woyvodich, Rebecca Yates-Campbell, Mary Ann Yewen, and Kim Zeigler.

I also want to thank those who saw the value in this book's concept, namely my exceedingly good agent Jacky Sach and the visionary team at Alpha Books/Penguin Group, especially Marie Butler-Knight, Randy Ladenheim-Gil, Dawn Werk, Megan Douglass, Rebecca Batchelor, Jennifer Moore, Billy Fields, Jaime Julian Wagner, and Laura Caddell.

Wine Basics

1

Trade Secrets

It's impossible to work in the wine trade and not learn a thing or two that initially surprises you because it runs counter to popular misconceptions, and then seems utterly reasonable when you stop to think about it. Let me give you some examples.

The wine trade teaches you that screw caps aren't just for cheap plonk—they work as well as corks for pretty much all wine. You learn that the expensive wines that critics wax lyrically over comprise a teensy portion of the market. Sure, a disproportionately large amount of ink spilled on the good stuff gives the illusion that everyone's drinking pricey bottles, but that's just not the case. It just means those wines have more budget to hire public relations professionals and to send out samples to wine critics. You also discover the best big-brand wines are made to taste the same every year, so vintage doesn't matter much. And that all wine under $20 is ready to drink upon bottling so there's no need to worry about aging it. Last but not least, you find makers are starting to put decent wine in boxes these days so you don't have to steer clear of this category entirely, although it's still prudent to tread carefully. I elaborate on each of these points in this chapter.

A Word on Screw Caps

Which is better, screw cap or cork? I would guess this debate has ruined more dinner parties than you can shake a corkscrew at. And now, with myriad other wine closures used for everyday, popular wines, the potential for more thunderingly boring discussions expands exponentially, as typified by the following exchange:

What do you think of screw caps?

Better than plastic stoppers but worse than corks.

You don't say. Why?

Well, screw caps are fine if the winemaker accounts for the wine's technical reaction to that closure during winemaking; otherwise, you end up with dreadful reductive notes ….

Reductive?

Dear God. Give me a drink! Is there anything more exhaustingly moisture-zapping than that type of talk? Give me politics, religion, anything … but not wine-bore debates.

To do my small part in preventing tedious discussions on wine closures beyond the confines of wine trade and science circles, I will end the debate right here. For the kinds of wines we're talking about in these pages, which are bottled young and fresh and meant for immediate consumption, any closure will do. The risk of tasting overbearing flavors of wet cardboard, glue, sulfur, or rotten egg from various wine flaws associated with closures are minimal. They can occur, sure. But the odds are pretty slim with the wines recommended in this book, which are among the most popular wines in the United States. If they were frequently badly tainted or terrible, they wouldn't be top-sellers—end of story.

That said, if you do find a wine tastes like any of the flavors I noted or is otherwise awful, don't drink it. Open your back-up bottle and carry on with your boat cruise, round of strip poker, or evening wind-down drink. Later, take the flawed bottle back to the shop and tell the clerk you think the wine is off. Get your money back, and try another bottle. Most retailers will accept a returned bottle on that basis, but if the merchant is unreasonable, take your business elsewhere.

A Word on Price

Price is a funny thing, and it gets downright comical when you start looking at price categories in the wine trade.

Wines that cost $3 to $5 are called *fighting varietals*— instant images pop up in my head of cockfights: bottles dressed up as roosters going at each other.

Go up a notch to $5 to $7.99 and you're into *premium* wine, which sounds fine until you get to the next two categories: $8 to $10.99 and $11 to $14.99, which are called *super premium* and *ultra premium*, respectively.

Good grief. Where do you go from there?

Well, $15 to $20 is considered *luxury*, and anything above that is *super luxury*.

Anything over $20 accounts for less than 3 percent of wine sales in the United States and shares one small category in the trade. That's right: all those wines you read about in *Wine Spectator* and elsewhere that cost $25, $45, or $105 comprise a puny portion of the market. Meanwhile, more than 90 percent of wines sold in the United States cost less than $15, which is why that price was my cutoff.

For the purposes of this book, we're sidestepping marketing-speak and using dollar signs to symbolize the four relevant per-bottle price brackets, translated into plain English here:

$	Super-low priced (under $4.99)
$$	Moderate ($5–$7.99)
$$$	Pricier ($8–$10.99)
$$$$	Splurge-worthy ($11–$15)

Prices do vary from state to state and from store to store, so I've used suggested retail prices to guide the placement of wines in this book. In cases where suggested retail price wasn't included with a wine sample, I categorized bottles based on their approximate retail values online at www.wine-searcher.com. This website lets you search for a specific wine by name and geographic area and then shows where it's available and at what prices. It's a useful way to comparison shop—retailers must hate it.

A Word on Vintage and Aging

One of the best things about popular big-brand wines is that they don't vary much from year to year. Like Big Macs, they are made to taste a certain way every time you have them—provided they are stored properly and drank within a few years of bottling. And to remind you not to worry about dates on bottles, I've omitted vintages entirely from the wines in this book. Sure, slight quality and flavor variation may occur year to year but the whole idea behind big brand wines is consistency. The winemakers shoot for a signature flavor profile, and have a toolbox of methods at hand in the winery to make that happen.

Although big brands taste pretty much the same year after year, always pick the latest vintage on the shelf. It's prudent to do so because all wines under $15 are cast out of the winery ready to drink and are made to be drunk young and fresh. This brings me to my next point: age-ability.

Storing a wine to let it improve in the bottle is a bad idea for at least 90 percent of wines on the market—and pretty much all the wines in this book. If a wine costs under $15, I guarantee it was made for immediate drinking. These wines may stay in their prime a little while—up to about six years from the vintage date on the bottle for red and up to about three years from that point for white or rosé (and I'm being very generous here)—but they won't improve. Like everything, there are exceptions to the rule. The odd $15 bottle of Cabernet Sauvignon or Syrah may improve with age but it will still be ready to drink upon bottling. I won't bore you with the technical reasons for this, but wines under $15 are not meant for aging. Buy them as you need them, keep them reasonably cool, and drink up. (For more on storing wines, see Chapter 2.)

A Word on Packaging

For years, bag-in-box wines were considered horrible, and generally, they were. The old technology didn't keep the wine fresh very long and the *vin* they put in boxes gave a whole new meaning to the term *vin ordinaire*—that French term for inexpensive table wine. But over the years, technology improved and better quality wine was packaged this way. You still have to tread carefully, but now we know bag-in-box wine can give you a perfectly satisfying glass.

The benefits are easy to see: bags-in-boxes give you a convenient way to drink cheap-and-cheerful wine over the course of days or weeks. They let you keep a variety of wines open at once without worry—maybe a red, white, and rosé. And they can stay fresh up to six weeks after opening instead of a couple of days or so for a bottle. Plus, they weigh less and obviously don't shatter.

Bag-in-box wine is the fastest growing wine packaging segment in the United States—not surprising when you taste some bag-in-box wines now on the market, the best of which are featured in this book. Here's to Château Cardboard!

2

Getting the Most Out of That Bottle

Did you know bright light can wreck a bottle of unopened wine within a few hours? Absolutely true. And serving a $10 bottle at the right temperature can make it taste like a $20 or even $30 wine. Without a doubt, how you store and serve a wine increases or decreases its pleasure dose dramatically. This chapter reveals secrets to take any wine up a notch and avoid common pitfalls.

Storing It

As noted earlier, all the wines in this book are bottled ready to drink. This means you don't have to worry about correct storage, right? Wrong. You can ruin an unopened bottle quickly by storing it incorrectly. The big wine enemies are: bright light, oxygen, heat, and dramatic temperature fluctuations. I'll explain each in turn.

Bright Light

It's a little-known fact light spoils wine. Bright light from the sun or a lightbulb can make wines smell of onion, cooked cabbage, wet wool, or wet dog—certainly not aromas most of us are looking for in that delicate Pinot Grigio.

A recent study that looked at the effects of light on wine showed that bottled wines placed about 2 feet from two 40-watt fluorescent lamps in a room at a constant temperature developed off aromas in just 3.3 hours in untinted bottles and 31 hours in tinted bottles. Most bottles are tinted for this reason, but many are not. All should be, frankly, to prevent them from acquiring so-called *light-struck* aromas and flavors.

Whites and rosés are more susceptible to light damage than reds because tannins inhibit the adverse reactions; and tannins—those naturally occurring compounds in grape skins, seeds, and stems that impart texture to wine—are found in far higher concentrations in reds than whites and rosés.

So it's best to store your bottles in the dark and avoid buying those that appear to have been basking in strong sunlight or close to bright lights at the shop.

Exposure to Oxygen

As soon as you open a bottle of wine, it starts to oxidize. This means that after about a day, wine begins to notice-ably lose its freshness because of the effects of oxygen. It will start to smell and taste a bit flat and stale instead of fresh and fruity. It will also show less articulate flavors and aromas and taste a little too sharp. Reds oxidize more slowly than whites and rosés, but all wine starts to decline once you open it.

There are a couple of ways around this. You can buy canisters of inert gas to squirt into leftover bottles; the gas blankets the wine's surface to block it from oxygen. This method actually works quite well, but you have to keep buying the cans of gas. The other contraption on the market is a fancy pump that vacuums the air out of the bottle to preserve the wine, but I'm not convinced this method works very well.

My favorite method for preserving leftover wine is to pour it into a smaller vessel—such as a half bottle—and re-cork it. Assuming the wine reaches the neck of the bottle, it won't be exposed to very much oxygen, so you're good for two or three more days. And the best place to store all leftover wine—red, rosé, or white—is in the refrigerator to slow down chemical reactions. Of course, if you're popping that red wine in the fridge, you'll want to take it out about 20 minutes before serving it to let it warm up a tad, as red wine should always be served slightly cooler than room temperature.

Heat

Heat speeds up all chemical reactions, including those that age wine. For a bottle that is at its peak—or "ready to drink," as they say—you don't want to accelerate the aging process or you send the wine into decline. Essentially, when a wine declines, the fruit falls out (meaning bright flavors dim), the alcohol can seem a little hot, and the whole experience becomes a lot less pleasant—so keep your bottles cool.

Dramatic Temperature Fluctuation

Storing wine in a place that warms up then cools down dramatically and repeatedly is another way to force a wine into decline. To prevent this, don't do things like store your bottles beside the stove or leave them in the garage when the days are 90°F and nights drop to 70°F. The odd chill won't affect them much, but too many temperature fluctuations are going to wreck your stash.

Serving It

How you serve a wine is as important as its inherent flavor. The fastest way to improve any bottle is by paying attention to the service temperature, glasses, food it's paired with, and drinking order.

Temperature

Although it strikes me as a bit tedious to use a thermometer to judge the exact temperature of a wine before the pour, it does make sense to pay attention to whether a wine is, say, room temperature, slightly chilled, or ice-cold, because you can seriously enhance a wine by serving it at the right temperature.

Color is the first clue. Most of us have heard that reds are best served at room temperature—but that old chestnut was around for eons, and no doubt it originally referred to the damp chill of a seventeenth century British country cottage or French château rather than the dry heat of the average centrally-heated home in the American suburbs. So the big mistake most people make is serving reds too warm, which makes the alcohol stand out rather than the fruit. A good rule of thumb is to put all reds in the fridge for 10 or 15 minutes before grabbing the corkscrew or twisting the cap. Lighter-bodied reds can chill a little longer than fuller-bodied ones to bring out their inherent refreshment factor.

Whites and rosés are best served a bit cooler than reds. How cold? Depends on the quality of the wine. The better the wine, the less you chill it. Low temperatures hide complexity, so you don't want to overchill better bottles—including, but not limited to, fine sparkling wines or complex wooded Chardonnays—or you'll lose everything that makes these wines great, and expensive. On the other hand, if a wine is simplicity itself, has been open a little too long, or is past its best, there's nothing to lose by serving it ice-cold, which will actually hide shortcomings such as little complexity, a bit of oxidation, or a lack of fruit.

Glasses

Does stemware matter? Absolutely. You can double the pleasure of any wine by drinking it from an appropriate glass. It doesn't even have to be expensive, really. It just has to be designed so that the rim's circumference is smaller than that of the bowl. This feature captures and concentrates a wine's aromas, making a wine seem more intense—and since the olfactory glands are far more sensitive than the taste buds, this feature is paramount. If you question the importance of your nose in wine appreciation, try tasting something with your nostrils pinched shut.

The other way to use glasses to improve wine is by choosing thin stemware. The thinner the glass, the finer the wine seems. Applying this principal is an effective way to take that vino up a few notches for a special occasion—and save a few dollars.

A huge range of shapes and sizes of wine glasses are on the market now, particularly by high-end companies specializing in designing shapes for every style of wine imaginable. While they do work to enhance the various types of wines, most of us don't have the cupboard space for more than a few wine glass styles. And really, there is no need to go overboard with stemware, as tempting as it may be. A set of larger glasses for reds, slightly smaller glasses for whites, and some flutes for bubblies should suffice. And if you like, have a set of each in finer glass or crystal for special occasions. I would even argue flutes are unnecessary; sparkling wine actually tastes better from white wine glasses because the broader surface area amplifies the all-important aromas.

Food

There are three basic principles of food and wine pairing, and they may surprise you.

While it's usually thought that a wine's color is the most important consideration when matching it to a dish, it's not. A wine's body is actually more significant. A full-bodied white such as a wooded Californian Chardonnay can hold up well to such heavy dishes as risotto, fried pork tenderloin, and even a cheeseboard—all of which are traditionally thought to be red wine partners. Meanwhile, a lighter-bodied Pinot Noir or Beaujolais can pair with salmon or poultry just as well as—or sometimes better than—many white wines. And here's a small pearl of wisdom: body can be determined by a quick glance at the label because it's closely related to alcohol level. Generally, you'll find a light-bodied wine has less than 12 percent alcohol, a medium-bodied wine has 12 to 13 percent alcohol, and a full-bodied one exceeds 13 percent alcohol.

The second principle of food and wine pairing is to match the flavor intensity of the dish with that of the wine. It's easier than you may think to obliterate the flavors and aromas of a wine. Obviously, a subtle and restrained Italian Pinot Grigio would be overpowered by grilled sausages, but it would also be overwhelmed by a salad with a too-flavorful dressing. For instance, a garlicky Caesar salad would be much better with a richly-fruited Chardonnay with a good punch of citrus flavor than a gently floral Pinot Grigio. If you think of the flavor intensity, rather than just the color, you'll find more satisfying selections.

The third big consideration is that a wine should always be as sweet as or sweeter than the food; otherwise, it will taste unpleasantly thin and acidic. A case in point: dry French Champagne with wedding cake. This pairing ruins the bubbly, which becomes searingly sour with the sugary dessert, and all the marvelous elegance and complexity you're paying for in the wine is lost. Better nuptial couplings would be Champagne with smoked salmon, and sweet sparkling wine, a dessert wine, or even just coffee with the cake. Some stellar wine-dessert matches include Port with chocolate tortes and cakes, Moscato with poached fruit, and Cream Sherry with cheese and figs. For savory-spicy-sweet entrées like Pad Thai, wines with some sweetness work best, such as off-dry Riesling or Gewürztraminer. These wines tend to be balanced with crisp, mouthwatering acidity to cleanse and cool the palate.

Drinking Order

Wine should always be consumed in the appropriate order, which is white and rosé before red, light before full-bodied, dry before sweet, and average before finer quality. And there are solid reasons for this thinking.

Moving from white to red and light-bodied to full lets the palate keep up with the progression. For a dinner party, this might mean serving a crisp sparkling wine as an aperitif, followed by asparagus spears and crab legs with a medium-bodied Sauvignon Blanc, and then rib-eye steak and fries with a top-notch Californian Cabernet. And sweet wines always follow dry to prevent the latter from seeming too austere. So this menu might end with a suculent, apricot-scented Late Harvest wine with a fresh fruit tart.

Serving the best quality bottles last guides the palate toward escalating pleasure. If you fall into the trap of pouring a great wine first, perhaps to showcase it before palates tire, lesser-quality bottles that follow bring no joy.

Tasting It

The business of wine tasting is a curious thing, actually. It's very different than wine drinking. When I taste a wine wearing my critic's cap, I pull apart the whole pleasure experience. I hold each aspect of the wine up against the cold yardstick of imaginary perfection. Is the fruit concentration and alcohol level in balance, or does the alcohol stand out too much? Does the wine taste appealingly crisp or searingly sour? Do the tannins taste velvety and ripe or stalky and green? Is the wine interestingly complex, resonating with five or more identifiable flavors and aromas, or does it seem rather one-dimensional and simple? And how is the typicity? In other words, does that Pinot Noir taste like a Pinot Noir—or like it's trying to be a Shiraz? There's no quiet conversation, eye-batting flirtation, suggestive comments, or even jazz. Instead, I'm alone in my home or with other studious wine critics in a lab setting with a spittoon in hand. Yes, I spit; inebriation wreaks havoc on tasting notes.

Bottom line: The whole process is rather clinical.

One could argue that tasting this way is too removed from the real drinking experience—and there may be something to be said for that. But there's serious value in technical wine tasting, and it's this: it can determine exactly why a wine does or doesn't taste good and therefore why you probably will or won't like it. Said another way, you might not know why you love or hate a wine but a wine critic probably would. The technical tasting process yields that insight on a bottle-by-bottle basis.

For instance, I pretty much guarantee you won't like a wine that's out of balance. If it has too much alcohol for the fruit, it will feel hot in your throat like a shot of vodka, which is not what most of us want in our Chardonnay. Or if it lacks fruit concentration compared to the acidity (a technical term that means sourness), the wine will seem thin and harsh. Bar none, everybody likes a wine that's balanced, and wine critics like me assess balance in a cold, calculated, academic way. Curiously, I get some kind of weird pleasure from the whole exercise—and if the banter that ricochets through trade tastings is any indication, other critics share this quirk.

Although all wines in this book have been tasted for technical correctness (because it makes a huge difference as to whether the wine is palatable or not), I've tried to steer clear of jargon in tasting notes. The point of this little volume is not to educate you on how to be a wine critic—that's why you've hired me by buying this book; rather it's to help you drink better wine. Tastier, more satisfying wine. Wine that overdelivers for the price. Wine that thrills.

Though you can't get that deep, gut-hysteria thing going without the right technical composition, the wine style and inherent flavors also have to appeal to you. You probably won't like the best Australian Cabernet-Shiraz if you like your wines delicate and light. You would have no idea why that restrained, herbaceous Sauvignon Blanc is considered great value at $15 if you prefer rich, vanilla-scented, oaked Chardonnay. And if you like tart lime? Drink Riesling. Like creamy vanilla? Drink oaked Chardonnay. Like blackcurrant? Drink Cabernet Sauvignon. Like "tinned" strawberries? Drink Pinot Noir.

To support the process of discovering which types of wines you like, I've explained exactly what each grape varietal tastes like in the first sentence or two of the relevant chapter. You can take it from there because if there's one truism to wine appreciation, it's this: tasting for pleasure is a very personal thing.

White Wines

FOLONARI

SOAVE

DENOMINAZIONE DI ORIGINE CONTROLLATA

3

White Blends

Blended wines can be fabulous. By blending different grape varieties, the winemaker swings the door wide open to possibility by controlling flavors, aromas, mouthfeel, body, sweetness, and acidity. The French call blending *assemblage*, which calls to mind the verb *assemble*. Essentially, blending wine layers flavors and textures to create something greater than the sum of the parts.

Although the advantages for less expensive wines are obvious—blending can seriously enhance a wine made from average fruit—even some of the most expensive white wines in the world are blends. Champagne makers routinely blend the elegance and delicacy of Chardonnay with the power and longevity of Pinot Noir before seasoning the wine with the tart, fruity vivacity of Pinot Meunier. And the top sweet wines of Sauternes in France are blends of Semillon and Sauvignon Blanc. Sadly, the term *blend* has come to suggest inferior wine, which is pure myth, as you'll discover when you taste some of the wines recommended in this chapter.

Lindemans Cawarra Semillon Chardonnay, South Eastern Australia

Sumptuous orange, bright lemon, and aromatic melon glaze the palate before finishing with a long, languid vanilla-nut-cream finish. Medium-bodied. 13% alc.

Folonari Soave DOC, Veneto, Italy

What a find! This charming little Italian blend of 80 percent Garganega and 20 percent Trebbiano is gently reminiscent of lime and cool, wet stones. Light- to medium-bodied. A classic, elegant dry wine everyone will enjoy. 12% alc.

WHITE BLENDS   **$$**

BEST

Riunite Bianco, Italy

Sassy lemon-floral-clementine flavors edged with honeyed apricot and chin-drip peaches. Some sweetness but perfectly balanced with cleansing acidity and surprisingly intense concentration. Great on its own or with spicy fare. Easy and light with just 8% alc. Just don't tell anyone the price!

Luna Di Luna Chardonnay Pinot Grigio, Italy

Feathery citrus-floral aromas move to fleeting brushstrokes of apple, peach, and gentle floral flavors. This 60 percent Chardonnay/40 percent Pinot Grigio in the cobalt blue bottle is an attractive, medium-bodied, midweek quaffer. 12% alc.

Mouton Cadet Blanc, Baron Philippe de Rothschild, Bordeaux AC, France

Perfect for those who prefer their wines a little less fruit-juicy, this classic Bordeaux blends Sauvignon Blanc, Semillon, and Muscadelle. It hints at mixed citrus on the nose before suggest-ing peaches, subtle floral notes and a certain mineral-ity reminiscent of crushed stones on the palate. Ulti-mately, this wine is about seductive restraint. Very French. Medium-bodied with 12% alc.

Truth in Labeling

The average 5-oz. glass of dry white wine has 82 calories and about 2.6 g carbohydrates according to the USDA. Calorie and carbohydrate counts vary considerably from wine to wine, and the federal government has proposed controversial legislation that would require producers to list nutritional information on wine labels. The legislation had not been ratified when this book went to print.

Big House White, California, USA

I love the interesting white cherry and rosewater aromas wafting from this pale straw wine. The sweet-talking bouquet leads to flavors of rose petal, white cherries, and kiwi fruit. Something about this wine reminds me of fresh, cotton sheets dried on the line, outdoors, in the sunshine. Dry, cool, crisp yet soft with considerable length. Lovely stuff. 13.5% alc.

What Is a Wine's "Length"?

A wine's length refers to the amount of time its flavor lingers in the mouth after you swallow. When flavors seem to disappear within a few seconds, the wine is said to be "short." When they seem to resonate for a full-minute or more, the wine is described as long, or as having "considerable length." Generally, long length is a hallmark of good quality in wine.

Banfi Fumaio Sauvignon Blanc & Chardonnay, Tuscany, Italy

This Tuscan blend shines silvery pale in the glass and exudes gentle floral aromas before a racy attack of grapefruit and honeydew melon zips across the palate. Medium-bodied and attractively labeled. 12.5% alc.

Folie à Deux Ménage à Trois White Table Wine, California, USA

Fragrant apricot and nectarine aromas lead to a titillating palate of juicy stone fruit, orange oil, and pear with a hint of steeliness. The three varieties in this ménage include Chardonnay, Moscato, and Chenin Blanc, each adding its own dimension to the overall appeal. Full-bodied. 13.5% alc.

BEST

Conundrum, White Table Wine, California, USA

This blend starts with fragrant honeysuckle and tangerine before attacking the palate with a good lick of Granny Smith apple, ripe apricot, and pear. Breezy, vivacious wine with a quick dash of spice and vanilla adding interest to the blend. Full-bodied and ripe. This cult wine is generally more than $15 per full bottle but the handy half-bottle size fits this price category.

Conundrum's Secret Blend
Unlike most wines in this book, Conundrum isn't made to a signature taste profile each vintage. Instead, it blends new proportions of the same five grape varieties each year, namely: Sauvignon Blanc, Chardonnay, Muscat Canelli, Semillon, and Viognier. Figuring out the exact blend could prove quite the conundrum.

4

Chardonnay

In its pure form, Chardonnay (pronounced *shar-don-NAY*) is crisp and refreshing with flavors and aromas reminiscent of apple, citrus, and tropical fruit. When aged or fermented in oak, the fruit becomes imbued with a warm creaminess that calls to mind vanilla, buttered toast, caramel, or warm spice notes.

It's fashionable to say you hate Chardonnay these days. Yet Chardonnay has been the leading wine grape in the United States for the last decade and sales increase every year. In fact, more than a quarter of all Californian wine sold in the United States is Chardonnay. It remains, bar none, the most planted, produced, and sought after varietal in the world and is made in almost every wine region on the planet.

Chardonnay is fascinating in its variability. Stylistically, Chardonnay swings from the austerity of fine French Chablis that attacks the palate with pure refreshment recalling the cool aroma of wet stones to the classic Californian style that caresses the tongue with fleshy, juicy tropical fruit and an unmistakable stroke of creamy vanilla from American oak. And between those extremes, every shade of Chardonnay imaginable exists.

In truth, it would be difficult to hate all types of Chardonnay.

The Little Penguin Chardonnay, South Eastern Australia

Sweet honey tangerine and nutty vanilla bean aromas lead to a lively palate that tastes quick and fresh with racing flavors of perfectly ripe melon and pineapple. This wine offers great purity of fruit before finishing with hints of warm bread and soft lemon cream. Full-bodied. 13.5% alc.

Leaping Horse Vineyards Chardonnay, Lodi, California, USA

This wine smells and tastes exactly like a lemon Danish pastry. Think bracing lemon curd, caramelized butter pastry, soft yeasted dough, and satisfying texture. Slightly off-dry, meaning it has a hint of sweetness, but well balanced with crisp acidity. It will almost certainly appeal to those with a weakness for lemon Danishes. Medium-bodied with 12.5% alc.

BEST

Lindemans Bin 65 Chardonnay, Australia

Glinting glossy, pale, lemon yellow in the glass, this bright fistful of pineapple and melon aroma and flavor is a bit creamy, a bit round—meaning it offers a pleasantly full weight in the mouth—and tastes just ripe and fruity enough to drink on its own or have with food. Medium-bodied. Well-balanced. 13% alc.

What's Your Wine Personality?
The Little Penguin website, www.thelittlepenguin.com, has a Wine Personality Test that reveals your ideal wine variety match and why.

A Toast to Chardonnay
No doubt about it—Chardonnay is huge. Americans drank the equivalent of 756 million 750 ml bottles of Chardonnay in 2008, and more than 85 percent of those Chardonnays were domestic.

Ideal Serving Temperature
The ideal serving temperature for Chardonnay varies dramatically. Simple, crisp, unoaked ones should be served very cold, perhaps straight from the fridge, while complex, creamy, oaked versions are best a few degrees warmer. Low temperatures hide subtle flavors and aromas, so let your nose and palate guide you when judging the best temperature to serve a Chardonnay.

Banrock Station Chardonnay, South Eastern Australia

Soft lemon curd and honeysuckle aromas lead to refreshing flavors of lemon, orange, and peach with a clean, crisp finish. This easy, satisfying drink is full-bodied with 13% alc.

Hardy's Stamp of Australia Chardonnay, South Eastern Australia

This vivid, surging Chardonnay is a fruity flirt of a wine. Orange oil and white peach purée flavors saturate the palate before toasty-creamy notes take over, recalling crème brûlée on the finish. Full-bodied. 13.5% alc.

BEST

Stone Cellars by Beringer Chardonnay, California, USA

This seriously seductive rendition of Californian Chardonnay shines pale golden in the glass. It exudes creamy coconut aromas before bathing the palate with sun-soaked fruit suggestive of pineapple, melon, and citrus topped with coconut cream. Dry and fruity, this wine's impeccable balance makes it seem incredibly rich and smooth. Delicious and seriously underpriced. Medium-bodied. 13% alc.

Beware!
Some Chardonnays can rise to 15 percent alcohol—and that's a lot. Anything over 13.5 percent alcohol will usually taste too hot in the throat, making it an unpleasant, out-of-balance drink. One of the best ways to cut the risk of dissatisfaction when buying Chardonnay is to check the alcohol level before you buy.

It's a Fact
Beringer is a reliable and respected name in Californian wine. In fact, Beringer Vineyards is the oldest continuously operating winery in Napa Valley, California.

WHITE

GOOD

BETTER

Penfolds Koonunga Hill Chardonnay, South Australia

Here's a classic, clean-cut, traditionally styled Aussie Chardonnay. Staggering amounts of ripe fruit flavors swirl around in this full-bodied wine, imbued with roasted almond, spice, and warm wood from maturing for several months in small French oak barrels called *barriques*. Long, creamy finish. 13.5% alc.

Cupcake Vineyards Chardonnay, Central Coast, California, USA

What a fitting name for this rich and creamy, vanilla-scented Chardonnay. Polished tropical fruit, integrated oak, and appealing notes of melting caramel combine with warm spice on the finish. Generous, soul-warming, comfort wine. Full-bodied with 13.5% alc.

CHARDONNAY $$$

Food Pairing
Great matches for gently-oaked Chardonnay include grilled salmon, chicken in cream sauce, and a cheeseboard of Gruyere, Havarti, and Camembert. It is also stellar with Caesar salad and broiled lobster tails with melted butter.

WHITE

BEST

Sterling Vintner's Collection Chardonnay, Central Coast, California, USA

This wine seems modeled on fine French Burgundies with their subtle power, taut fruit, and judicious use of oak. Buttered toast nose leads to flavors of lemon zest, cooked apple, and fresh figs with a topcoat of caramel and spice. Full-bodied with 13.5% alc.

Mezzacorona Estate Bottled Chardonnay, Vigneti Delle Dolomiti IGT, Italy

From the northern reaches of Italy, this cool, crisp, gently-oaked Chardonnay suggests bright apple butter on oven-warm bread with subtle hints of toasty oak. It's a bit more restrained than most New World renditions of this grape variety, making it a terrific food wine. Medium-bodied. 13% alc.

Concannon Vineyard Chardonnay, Central Coast, California, USA

Appealing pink grapefruit and creamy mango flavors threaded through with notes of vanilla, cinnamon, and nutmeg. Well-balanced and full-bodied. 13.5% alc.

BEST

Cavit Collection Chardonnay, Trentino DOC, Italy

This unoaked Chardonnay is all about Old World subtlety and could even be mistaken for a well-made Pinot Grigio. Lean, clean, tart pear and apple flavors wrap around a tight mineral core. What a marvelous, silky wine to go with oven-warmed brie and walnuts! Medium-bodied with 12.5% alc.

The Wine-Music Connection
Upbeat pop tunes can make Chardonnay taste more "zingy and refreshing," according to recent findings from researchers at Hariot-Watt University in Edinburgh. The results were attributed to *cognitive priming theory*, meaning music sets up the brain to respond to wine in a certain way.

Bogle Vineyards Chardonnay, California, USA

This wine starts with an incredibly enticing aroma of crème brûlée before zipping across the palate with a ripe, crisp, and full-on attack of juicy pear, cooked apple, and cream. Hints of vanilla, caramel, oak, and nutmeg add interest to this full-bodied wine with 13.5% alc., making this a solid value from a reliable producer.

Catena Alamos Chardonnay, Mendoza, Argentina

This Chardonnay offers seriously good value for the money with its ripe, rich, citrus-laden expression of fruit layered with subtle floral-spice-vanilla nuances. Full-bodied yet well proportioned. 13.5% alc.

BEST

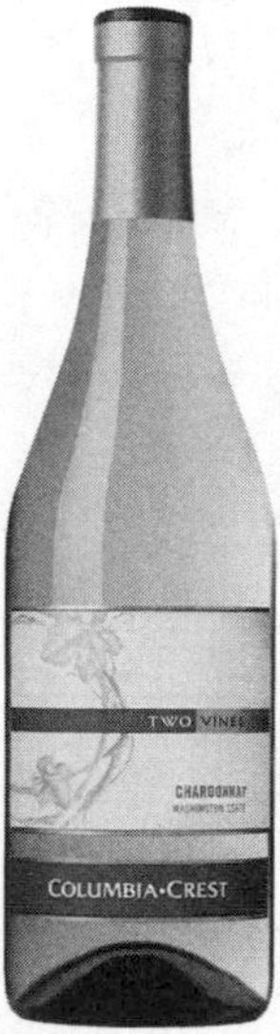

Columbia Crest Two Vines Chardonnay, Washington State, USA

An incredibly supple, sophisticated Chardonnay that charms the nose and palate with lively citrus notes of orange peel and grapefruit underpinned with well-integrated, understated nuttiness from oak. An excellent, full-bodied wine, offering tremendous value. 13.5% alc.

History Lesson
Chardonnay is an ancient grape variety thought to have originated in Lebanon—not France, which is widely considered the grape's heartland today.

Clos du Bois Chardonnay, North Coast, California, USA

This creamy, ripe style of Chardonnay delivers fresh flavors and aromas of caramel apple, juicy pear, and bright lemon as well as fleeting notes of butter and toasty oak. Full-bodied and quite classic wine with 13.5% alc.

Columbia Crest Grand Estates Chardonnay, Columbia Valley, Washington State, USA

Delicate orange blossom aromas waft from the glass, leading to focused flavors of crisp apple and poached pear. Mouth-filling fruit is nuanced with vanilla and buttered toast before tapering to a long, warm toffee finish. Full-bodied with 13.5% alc.

BEST

Kendall-Jackson Vintner's Reserve Jackson Estates Grown Chardonnay, California, USA

Coconut and tropical fruit cocktail nose leads to fresh flavors of juicy pineapple, marzipan, and toasted coconut. Long and seductive coconut cream finish. Seamlessly integrated oak and pristine purity of fruit create quite a stylish, refined wine. Full-bodied and beautifully balanced. 13.5% alc.

WHITE

Burgundy's Chardonnay

Though it's generally agreed among wine experts that Burgundy makes some of the finest Chardonnay in the world, you won't find the grape variety printed on the labels. It's actually illegal for the best wines of that region to do so because in France, the wine laws that govern top wine production put place of origin above all else. So you see the region, district, commune, or vineyard names on Burgundian labels instead of grape varietals. The premise is that place of origin matters more than grape variety because a wine, from the French perspective, is a product of its "terroir"—which is the compilation of geographic place, climate, weather, grape, and soil. It is also assumed that wine drinkers know the grapes permitted by French law to be grown in any given demarcated area in France.

Pinot Grigio

Pinot Grigio (pronounced *pee-no GREE-gee-oh*) is a petal-light wine with feathery strokes of lemon-lime and floral notes.

Despite the fact wine snobs scorn Pinot Grigio for being too neutral, too bland, and much too characterless to be taken seriously, Americans love Pinot Grigio. In the last five years or so, its popularity has skyrocketed. It's the most popular imported wine in America—and why not? While much of it may be neutral, some of it is simply clean, elegant, honest refreshment. And the best Pinot Grigio possesses a gentle floral-stony character rather than simply featureless fruit.

But Pinot Grigio isn't new. Italians have been drinking it for years all over the old boot. They tend to drink it with fish from waters off the eastern seaboard because it's a perfect pairing; Pinot Grigio's understated nature doesn't upstage seafood with strong flavors and aromas.

While some of the finest Pinot Grigio still comes from Italy, New World producers from California and Australia are making some outstanding versions, too—as you'll discover in this chapter.

Here's to Pinot Grigio!

GOOD

BETTER

[yellow tail] Pinot Grigio, South Eastern Australia

Creamy lemon-almond aromas lead to a refreshing palate of zingy lemons and zesty lime. With generous fruit, an accessible style, and a bright seam of mouthwatering acidity, this wine is the definition of easy drinking. Medium-bodied with 12.5% alc.

Woodbridge by Robert Mondavi Pinot Grigio, California, USA

This is outrageously good value wine that walks the line between traditional Italian restraint and more flamboyant Californian fruit. A pronounced almost-sweet aroma of lemons and limes takes the lead before charming the palate with floral, orange, and warm spice cake flavors wrapped in a silky, seamless mouthfeel. Light- to medium-bodied with 12% alc.

Ideal Serving Temperature
40°F—think straight out of the fridge.

BEST

Citra Pinot Grigio IGT, Sicily, Italy

This pale yellow wine with subtle green reflections starts with a captivating whiff of white peach and lemon blossom before moving to a racy palate of lime zest and tart lemon sorbet. Taut acidity gives a refreshing edge of tartness to the fruit of this well-balanced wine, offering solid value from a traditional Italian producer. Medium-bodied. 12.5% alc.

Castello di Gabbiano Pinot Grigio, delle Venezie IGT, Italy

For archetypal Pinot Grigio with pedigree you can taste, reach for this bottle from a winery established in 1124—that's about 885 years ago. This pale, straw-colored wine starts with a subtle spring garden nose then leads to a lean palate of citrus, honeydew melon, and cantaloupe. Wiry acidity threads through tightly-wound fruit. Medium-bodied. 12.5% alc.

Mezzacorona Pinot Grigio, Vigneti Delle Dolomiti IGT, Italy

This glossy, pale, straw-colored wine shows restraint on the nose, suggesting only the lightest strokes of lemon before sliding across the palate with sleek flavors of fresh, creamy lime sherbet and a hint of smoke. Fresh and nervy wine with dry minerals on the finish. Easy crowd-pleaser from a reliable producer. Medium-bodied with 12.5% alc.

BEST

Nutritional Information
The average 5-oz. glass of Pinot Grigio contains 122 calories and 3.02 g carbohydrates.

Smell Smoke?
Pinot Grigios from the sub-alpine Trentino-Alto Adige region of northern Italy can taste a smidge smoky, which can be quite appealing. Mezzacorona Pinot Grigio is one such example.

Cavit Collection Pinot Grigio, Delle Venezie IGT, Italy

This little number exudes breezy wildflower aromas before seducing the senses with racy lemon-lime and pink grapefruit flavors. Graceful, elegant, and very Italian. But the real magic of this wine is its incredible texture—pure spun silk. A seriously good Pinot Grigio and one for your must-try list, although you may already know it because it's one of the best-selling Pinot Grigios in America. Light-to medium-bodied with 12% alc.

May I Take Your Order?
The most popular Pinot Grigio sold in United States' restaurants is Cavit, followed by Ecco Domani, Mezzacorona, and Santa Margherita, according to *Restaurant Wine* magazine.

$$$$ PINOT GRIGIO

Loredona Pinot Grigio, Monterey, California

Shining pale straw in the glass, this polished wine offers creamy lemon curd aromas before attacking the palate with sliced pear and pretty honeysuckle notes. Unlike more traditional renditions of Pinot Grigio, this wine is oaked, creating a warm vanilla flavor that lingers on the finish. Full-bodied with 13.5% alc.

Ecco Domani Pinot Grigio, delle Venezie IGT, Italy

This is an outstanding Pinot Grigio. Pale-colored straw with golden reflections in the glass, it exudes seductive dry-roasted cashew and Brazil nut aromas then hits the palate with flavors of hazelnut as well as tight lemon and pineapple. With seamless texture and bracing acidity, this wine offers great value. Medium-bodied with 12.5% alc.

PINOT GRIGIO $$$$

BEST

Mirassou Pinot Grigio, California, USA

Quite a sophisticated Pinot Grigio for the price with lots of interesting minerality that connoisseurs love. This wine starts with aromas of lime sorbet and crushed stones before charming the palate with racy lime, lemon, and pear flavors over a firm mineral core. It finishes with a long, appealing, slightly bitter note of lime zest. Astonishingly good value for the money. 13.5% alc.

Trade Secrets
Ecco Domani is the best-selling Pinot Grigio over $9 in America.

A Bit of History
The Mirassou family has been growing wine grapes in sunny California since 1854, earning it the distinction of being America's oldest winemaking family.

It's a Fact!
Pinot Grigio grapes range from bluish-grey to brownish-pink, traditionally producing a rusty-colored or slightly pinkish wine. In 1961, Santa Margherita became the first winery to use the grapes to make a pure white wine. They did so by limiting the grape skins' contact with the juice to avoid acquiring color—a technique perfected by the French in Champagne. Now most Pinot Grigios are quite pale white wines.

Sauvignon Blanc/ Fumé Blanc

Sauvignon Blanc (pronounced *sew-vin-yawn BLONK*) refreshes like a thing possessed. Mouthwateringly green strokes of flavor attack the palate like no other, recalling damp herbs, asparagus, cut grass, lime, and gooseberry. Fumé Blanc (pronounced *foo-may BLONK*) is another name for Sauvignon Blanc.

These wines lift salads, pestos, fish dishes, and herbed chicken the way a perfectly tailored Armani jacket elevates and finishes an outfit, yet they don't generally cost a fortune. And Sauvignon Blanc and asparagus is a combination as perfect as Oreos and milk, potatoes and sour cream, or spaghetti and tomato sauce. Sauvignon Blanc's natural lime-squirt acidity refreshes the palate between mouthfuls of oily or buttery dishes, making it a great food wine— and you can't find a better cocktail alternative than the gooseberry-drenched versions from Marlborough, New Zealand. Marlborough Sauvignon Blanc with its full-throttle fruit bumps almost all other wines to take top place for quintessential quencher.

In short, the best Sauvignon Blancs are wonderfully balanced spheres of flavor that roll around on your tongue and tickle your fancy in the most titillating way. To see what I mean, try a few bottles recommended in this chapter.

Pepperwood Grove Sauvignon Blanc, California, USA

Wafting aromas of red and green apple lead to a generous attack of crisp Granny Smith flavors edged with fresh basil. Perfect accompaniment to a wide range of foods. Full-bodied with 13.5% alc.

CK Mondavi Family Vineyards Willow Springs Sauvignon Blanc, California, USA

Candied orange peel aromas combine with unmistakable flavors of orange oil and grapefruit imbued with hints of green bell pepper. Medium-bodied with a long lemon and orange oil finish. 12.5% alc.

SAUVIGNON BLANC/FUMÉ BLANC $$

BEST

Woodbridge by Robert Mondavi Sauvignon Blanc, California, USA

A fresh, fruit-juicy style of Sauvignon Blanc with lively aromas of gooseberry and green pea that echo on the palate, layered with pear and kiwi. Impeccable balance. Medium-bodied with 13% alc.

A.K.A. Fumé Blanc

In the late 1960s, wine-maker Robert Mondavi noticed that Americans loved the French Sauvignon Blanc called Pouilly Fumé and were starting to look for drier wines to accompany food. Meanwhile, the Californian Sauvignon Blanc of the day was sweet and rather ordinary. So Mondavi began fermenting Sauvignon Blanc dry and aging it in oak barrels. Then, he renamed the new style, Fumé Blanc. Voilà—a success!

Other producers make Fumé Blanc now, but it's not always oaked. Instead, it is often made in the French Loire Valley style that encourages clean mineral and quiet herbal notes or in the Bordeaux Blanc style that blends in Semillon to create more weight in the mouth and cut the sharp acidity of pure Sauvignon Blanc. But Robert Mondavi is recognized as the first to coin the term Fumé Blanc.

Food Pairing

Sauvignon Blanc and a bucket of fried chicken.

Kendall-Jackson Vintner's Reserve Sauvignon Blanc, California, USA

This dry, aromatic wine shows chiseled flavors and aromas of ripe melon, tart lime, and juicy fig. Quite rich and full-bodied with mouthwatering acidity to cleanse the palate. 13.5% alc.

Fetzer Vineyards Valley Oaks Sauvignon Blanc, California, USA

Fleeting aromas of grapefruit and cut grass lead to a full-bodied, racy palate of Granny Smith apples, pink grapefruit, and sweet apricots. Smooth, highly toned texture and meticulous balance. 13.5% alc.

SAUVIGNON BLANC/FUMÉ BLANC **$$$**

BEST

Rosemount Diamond Label Sauvignon Blanc, South Eastern Australia

Pronounced asparagus and lime zest on the nose lead to a crisp yet silky palate that's citrusy yet herbal, full but delicate, lean yet muscular. Medium-bodied and balanced. Impressive. 12.5% alc.

Sauvignon Blanc's Many Aliases

The finest French Sauvignon Blancs from the Loire Valley are called Sancerre (pronounced *sawn-SARE*) and Pouilly Fumé (pronounced *poo-wee foo-MAY*). These wines come from the regions of the same names and their distinguishing feature is a deeply mineral character that recalls the scent of stones or flint. Imagine walking along wet rocky shores on a damp day or flint striking steel. This minerality makes connoisseurs swoon.

Nutritional Information

The average 5-oz. glass of Sauvignon Blanc contains 128 calories and 3.0 g carbohydrates.

Kenwood Vineyards Sonoma County Sauvignon Blanc, Sonoma County, California, USA

Mouth-filling flavors of apple and lime broaden to include hints of juicy grapefruit, lemongrass, and honeydew melon. A touch tropical. Intense fruit concentration is anchored with razor-sharp acidity wrapped in a supple mouthfeel. Full-bodied. 13.5% alc.

Starborough Marlborough Sauvignon Blanc, Marlborough, New Zealand

Aromatic gooseberry nose leads to a full punch of green apple, gooseberry, and asparagus flavor. Wines like this one are what put Marlborough on the map with its stunning rendition of Sauvignon Blanc. Lovely, ripe, and refreshing medium-bodied wine. Can't buy a better aperitif for the price. 12.5% alc.

SAUVIGNON BLANC/FUMÉ BLANC $$$$

BEST

Dancing Bull Sauvignon Blanc, California, USA

Bottled restraint. Attractive aromas of minerals and damp herbs lead to an incredibly smooth palate of cool, wet stones and mild greens. Quite refined, delicate, and suggestive of the finer bottles of the Loire Valley in France. An incredible value. 13.5% alc.

Try It Again

If you didn't like Californian Sauvignon Blanc years ago and have been avoiding it ever since, try it again. In the '60s, Californian Sauvignon Blanc was aggressive with sharp cut-grass flavors. As Americans embraced oaked Chardonnays in the '90s, the fashion in Sauvignon Blanc followed suit and it became rounder, softer, and less overtly green. These days, wine drinkers want refreshing wines, and we're seeing Californian Sauvignon Blancs become more tart with herbaceous notes showing through—yet they're more restrained and refined than those of the 1960s.

WHITE

Clos du Bois Sauvignon Blanc, North Coast, California, USA

This very pale, almost silvery wine exudes soft snow pea and freshly-cut green apple aromas before blasting the palate with racy gooseberry, green apple, and tart lime sorbet. Long, slow, lime finish. 13.5%

Kim Crawford Marlborough Sauvignon Blanc, Marlborough, New Zealand

Seriously explosive gooseberry, passion fruit, and asparagus on the nose and palate. Generously broad yet bracing wine with quick lime-squirt acidity. Exciting and invigorating with a medium-bodied weight of 13% alc.

BEST

**Robert Mondavi Winery
Fumé Blanc, Napa Valley,
California, USA**

Distinct aroma of a freshly
sharpened pencil on the
nose suggests an elegance
that's confirmed on the palate. Delicate damp herbs,
cool wet stones, and subtle
pencil shavings from the
light contact with oak imbue the softly refreshing
palate. Sheer pleasure. Deceivingly full-bodied. This
is what Fumé Blanc is all
about. 14.5% alc.

WHITE

7

Riesling

Riesling (pronounced *REESE-ling*) tastes of lime. It can suggest lime oil, lime sorbet, lime zest, but always lime, sometimes overlaid with hints of kerosene (a classic scent associated with maturing Riesling), minerals, and steel.

Riesling is the darling of wine connoisseurs—no doubt about it. The wine trade is charmed by Riesling's ability to range from bone dry to lusciously sweet without losing its balance. Even the sugariest versions don't cloy—like tipping back a glass of liquid honey would—because the grape's natural tartness offsets any sweetness and cleanses the palate.

This matter of sweetness brings me to an important point. America thinks dry and drinks sweet. Though most people will tell you they prefer dry wines, the most popular bottles in the United States do contain some residual sugar; they taste dry because sourness hides sweetness. That means you probably have no idea when you're drinking a slightly sweet wine because it's balanced with enough sourness—or acidity—to simply seem round and caressingly delicious while finishing dry. Take away acidity and you start to notice the sugar.

To get a first-hand lesson in what I'm talking about, taste any of the wines in this chapter. Most will seem quite dry but, technically, few actually are; they are just perfectly balanced.

GOOD

BETTER

Woodbridge by Robert Mondavi Riesling, Mosel, Germany

Sweet poached apricots and freshly rolled pastry on the nose lead to an attack of ripe apples, lime, and butter pastry again. Polished mineral underpinnings. Well-balanced and light-bodied with 11% alc.

Jacob's Creek Riesling, South Eastern Australia

This straw-colored wine with glints of green exudes aromas of lime and kerosene before ripping across the palate with explosive flavors of juicy lime and crisp green apple. A very clean, very bright, accessible wine. Tart and balanced. Medium-bodied with 13% alc.

WHITE

BEST

Fünf
5
german riesling

Fünf 5 German Riesling, Germany

Quiet candied lime peel aromas lead to an intense, tangy blast of mouth-filling lemon-lime sorbet. Medium sweet but impeccably balanced with sharp acidity so it finishes dry. Tantalizing and refreshing with serious fruit concentration. Fun stuff to drink on its own or with spicy food. And at a light-bodied 9% alc., feel free to gulp.

Serving Temperature for Riesling
45°F is about right for Riesling—5 or 10 degrees warmer than the average refrigerator. You don't want to serve Rieslings straight from the fridge because that level of chill will hide all that marvelous complexity for which this varietal is famous. Meanwhile, you want to serve it cool enough to play up its hallmark crispness.

Nutritional Information
The average 5-oz. glass of Riesling contains 118 calories and 5.54 g carbohydrates.

J. Lohr Estates Bay Mist Monterey White Riesling, Monterey County, California, USA

This glossy, pale, straw-colored wine with muted aromas attacks the palate with vibrant lime before evolving toward red grapefruit and juicy, ultra-ripe pear followed by soft honeydew melon. Well-balanced and medium-bodied with 13% alc.

Relax Riesling, Mosel, Germany

The attractive sea salt and lemon aromas of this pale, straw-colored wine are followed by incredibly concentrated flavors of bright lime and firm minerals overlaid with heady flavors of juicy peach and crisp apple. Off-dry but finishes dry. Light-bodied, sleek, accessible wine with 9.5% alc.

WHITE

BEST

Cavit Collection Riesling, Provincia di Pavia IGT, Italy

This pale and shiny Italian Riesling starts with cool restraint—a gently mineral nose—then moves to a delicate and elegant palate of dry stones, subtle lime, and lime blossoms. Quite sophisticated, light-bodied, and reasonably priced. 11.5% alc.

Top Dollar
Germany is the heartland of great Riesling, with the Mosel region spinning out arguably the most admirable bottles in the world. And while German Rieslings are the bargains of the wine world today, that wasn't always the case. In the late 1800s, German Rieslings fetched higher prices than top red Bordeaux, which are the most expensive bottles on the market today.

Jacob's Creek Reserve Riesling, South Australia

Here, fresh lemon-lime flavors and aromas are layered with attractive jasmine and mineral notes while the intense fruit concentration offsets taut acidity to create impeccable balance. This wine is a very simple answer to a wide range of dishes and occasions. Medium-bodied at 12% alc.

Chateau Ste. Michelle Dry Riesling, Columbia Valley, Washington State, USA

This rather austere, mineral style of Riesling with lean lime, green apple, and cantaloupe flavors and aromas is a versatile wine for food pairing. Well-balanced, crisp, and medium-bodied with 13% alc.

RIESLING $$$$

BEST

Food Pairings
Riesling's lime-squirt acidity and relatively light body makes it an excellent quaffer for spicy fare such as Szechuan dishes, sizzling stir-fries, or even Jamaican jerk chicken.

WHITE

Kendall-Jackson Vintner's Reserve Riesling, California, USA

Starting with warm lime and sunny stone fruit aromas, this pale gold wine offers quite a lot of richness on the palate with stewed peaches, tangerine, and ripe pear edged with gentle floral nuances suggesting orange blossom. An unusual rendition of the variety but captivating indeed. It's very well-balanced, round and lush, and finishes dry. Medium-bodied with 13% alc.

Did You Know?
The finest Rieslings in the world are capable of enormous aging potential. They can continue to improve in bottle for decades when cellared properly, which is quite a long time for a white wine.

73

8

Other Great Whites

Though the big four varieties—Chardonnay, Pinot Grigio, Sauvignon Blanc, and Riesling—are what most people drink most of the time in the United States, white wine is made from a wide range of other grapes, too—and some are swoon-worthy. The peachy-pear scented Viognier, the lychee- and rose-infused Gewürztraminer, the intoxicatingly floral-crisp Albariño. The sunny Muscats, stony Muscadets, and friendly Pinot Blancs. And let's not forget South Africa's Chenin Blanc, Austria's Grüner Veltliner, and Argentina's Torrontés.

This chapter is a nod and a wink to all the glorious white wines outside that tight clique of more popular grape varieties. These are the wines with regional appeal, open-handed generosity of flavor, and intriguing—if less traditional—beauty. Unlike the other wines in this book, they weren't compared to one another but rather were judged on technical correctness, balance, and unabashed capacity to please.

Pepperwood Grove Viognier, California, USA

Attractive aromas of peach, almond, and lemongrass lead to warm flavors of stewed stone fruit, grapefruit, and clove. Full-bodied with 13.5% alc.

Citra Trebbiano d'Abruzzo, Abruzzo, Italy

A nose of talcy minerals leads to a crisp, refreshing palate imbued with delicate pear and floral notes. The result is a tight harmony of aromas and flavors in this refreshing and beautifully balanced wine. Lighter side of medium-bodied with 12% alc.

BEST

WHITE

Sutter Home Family Vineyards Moscato, California, USA

Pronounced aromas of sweet marmalade and succulent stewed peaches lead to a seductive palate of luscious stone fruit and citrus zest. The sweet fruit is threaded through with enough acidity to create perfect balance so it finishes dry. Outstanding value dessert wine but also a lovely aperitif served chilled in the afternoon. And while the sweetness makes this wine seem full-bodied, it's actually quite light in alcohol with 9.5% alc.

Ruffino Orvieto Classico DOC, Umbria, Italy

This little Italian number is a great alternative to Pinot Grigio or unwooded Chardonnay with its restrained, crisp nature and captivating flavors of lemon blossom, Golden Delicious apple, cantaloupe, and almond. It's a medium-bodied classic with 12.5% alc. that's very versatile with food!

Trapiche Varietals Torrontés, Mendoza, Argentina

Aromas of lychees and roses move to a lively, citrus-floral attack and orange and grapefruit rind finish. This wine is all about tightly-coiled concentration and long length while maintaining impeccable balance and optimal refreshment. Great value. Full-bodied with 13.5% alc.

BEST

Barefoot Cellars "Deliciously Sweet" Moscato, California, USA

The label is right; this wine is deliciously sweet. Aromatic flavors of wildflowers and rose, luscious apricot, and succulent citrus oil are balanced by a bright seam of vibrant acidity. Incredible value wine to serve with dessert or the cheeseboard—or as dessert itself. While this wine's sweetness makes it taste quite full-bodied, it's light in alcohol with 9% alc.

WHITE

What Is Orvieto?

Orvieto is an Italian wine produced near the medieval city of the same name in Umbria. Although it can often be bland and uninteresting, Ruffino's version is fragrant and fairly complex, based on a mix of local Grechetto, Procanico, Verdello, and Canaiolo Bianco winegrapes.

Nutritional Information

The average 5-oz. glass of Moscato contains 129 calories and 7.85 g carbohydrates.

Feudo Arancio Grillo, Sicily IGT, Italy

Steely nose leads to a restrained palate reminiscent of jasmine, lemons, lemon blossoms, stones, and apples. Dry lime finish. A delicate, versatile, refined wine with medium body and 13% alc.

Ironstone Vineyards Obsession Symphony, California, USA

Pale yellow in color, this Californian variety—Symphony is the grape—smells slightly confected, suggesting candied citrus peel and spiced peach, before sliding across the palate with white grapefruit, lemon oil, honeysuckle, spiced peach, and ripe pear. Off-dry and light- to medium-bodied with 12% alc.

OTHER GREAT WHITES $$$

Nutritional Information
The average 5-oz. glass of Gewürztraminer contains 119 calories and 3.83 g carbohydrates.

Fetzer Vineyards Valley Oaks Gewürztraminer, California, USA

Classic scents of lychees and rosebuds lead to an off-dry palate with balancing acidity. Concentrated flavors of lychee, peach, white cherry, and spice. Outstanding rendition of this grape variety. Medium-bodied with 12% alc.

Martín Códax Albariño, Rías Baixas DO, Spain

Fresh lime and floral scents lead to a taut, refreshing palate of lime blossoms, soft lemon, almond, and apple with hints of green herbs. Restrained, complex, and versatile. Medium-bodied with 13% alc.

Trapiche Broquel Torrontés, Mendoza, Argentina

Gentle white pepper nose leads to an elegant palate of restrained citrus oil, stone fruit, and spice. It evolves in the mouth toward notes of fresh ginger, thyme, and bay leaf. Intriguing match for a range of dishes from baked chicken to fresh warm goat cheese on mixed greens. Full-bodied. 13.5% alc.

OTHER GREAT WHITES $$$$

BEST

Loredona Viognier, Lodi, California, USA

Fragrant nose of super-ripe apricots and stewed pears leads to off-dry apricot, lilac, orange blossom, nectarine, and tangerine flavors with a whisper of spice on the finish. This is a crisp, quenching, and almost creamy-tasting wine that's quite complex, full-bodied, and attractively labeled. Stylish stuff. 13.5% alc.

Albariño (pronounced *alba-REE-no*) ...

... is the flagship grape variety of Rías Baixas, Spain, and is rather fashionable right now. Albariño calls to mind bitter almond, flowers, and green apples. The most notable feature of Albariño is its hallmark bracing acidity, making it taste quite fresh. Grilled or sautéed scallops are the perfect food match.

Torrontés (pronounced *tore-rahn-TEZ*) ...

... is Argentina's signature white grape that produces crisp and dry—yet fruity— wines. Nuances range from lime and orange to peach and flowers. Often, there's an appealing mineral character that suggests wet stones.

What's Hot?

Viognier (pronounced *vee-OHN-yay*) is becoming an increasingly popular grape, with significant plantings in France, Australia, and the United States. This varietal produces dry, aromatic whites that taste of peaches and pear.

83

Red Wines

9

Red Blends

Three beauties who resemble Brando, Beckham, and Banderas—or Bardot, Kidman, and Jolie, if you prefer—are each obviously more than fine alone but together they're a fierce, light-up-the-night charm squad. It's alchemy. The halo effect. More than the sum, as it goes. And it's the same with red wine; a good blend can improve the overall package.

A coarse Cabernet Sauvignon seems smoother with Merlot. A rich, chocolaty Shiraz gets a spike of juicy freshness from Grenache. And a sassy but simple Sangiovese—the grape of Chianti—gains sophistication and complexity with a dash of Cabernet Sauvignon.

Blending is exciting stuff, and winemakers really get into it, manipulating more than flavor, aroma, and acidity; they play with tannin—that tongue-gripping, gum-drying quality that in the best cases feels like supple, crushed velvet in the mouth. Imagine the plush vest of some eighteenth-century royal in full regalia—not that you would be pressing your tongue against it. Or maybe you would; I don't know. Point is, winemakers toy with tannins to strive for textural nirvana.

Technical stuff aside, blending boils down to one thing: better wine at better prices. Just taste a few of the bottles recommended in this chapter. You'll see.

The Little Penguin Cabernet-Merlot, South Eastern Australia

This bold blend strikes a great balance between generous fruit-bomb-appeal and sufficient structure in the form of tannic grip and mouthwatering acidity, meaning it can swing from cocktail alternative to food wine quite easily. Ripe plum, blackcurrant, and cherry aromas and flavors predominate in this full-bodied wine with 13.5% alc.

Jacob's Creek Shiraz Cabernet, South Eastern Australia

With a full flush of concentrated plum, cherry, and blackberry flavor with hints of smoke, cedar, and green bell pepper, this wine tastes tight, bright, and smooth. Full-bodied with 14% alc.

BEST

It's Huge
Jacob's Creek is one of the most popular wine brands in Australia, producing about 7 million cases of wine each year.

[yellow tail] Shiraz-Grenache, South Eastern Australia

This wine is the equivalent of award-winning, gourmet barbecue sauce—and I mean that in the best possible way. Smoky, concentrated, and ripe with a generous kick of spice, it's an easy crowd-pleaser. Full-bodied with 13.5% alc. It's really not surprising this is one of America's favorite wines.

Warning
[yellow tail] is not for those who prefer a bone-dry, less fruit-forward style of wine. But those who like this round, fleshy, sweet-fruited style like [yellow tail] a lot!

RED

[yellow tail] Cabernet-Merlot, South Eastern Australia

Chock full of sweet berry fruit, this broad, juicy wine heaves with aromas and flavors of ripe wild cherry and cassis before finishing with a final shot of creamy coffee. Full-bodied with 13.5% alc.

[yellow tail] Shiraz-Cabernet, South Eastern Australia

Loads of sweet, jammy, berry flavors with notes of smoldering charcoal, black peppercorn, and dried herbs. Round with a hint of grip on the tongue, and well worth the money. Full-bodied with 13.5% alc.

BEST

**Big House Red, California,
USA**

Subtle berry aromas lead to
a riveting attack of mixed
berry flavors layered with
leather, chocolate, smoke,
and a warm meatiness with
an earthy undertow. This
seriously complex and
seamless blend of 10 red
grape varieties tastes lifted
and stylish rather than
heavy and brawny, finish-
ing with a dark chocolaty
finish that feels polished to
a high sheen. Full-bodied
with 13.5% alc.

RED

Red Truck Red Wine, California, USA

This gutsy blend of 41% Syrah, 30% Petite Sirah, 20% Cabernet Franc, and 9% Merlot swells with flavors of tightly-packed berries, peppercorn, and a hint of that cherry cough syrup you liked as a kid. Full-bodied with 13.5% alc.

Folonari Bardolino DOC, Veneto, Italy

This traditional blend of local grape varieties—Corvina, Rondinella, Molinara, and Negara—has very little aroma but rips across the palate with spirited red cherry flavors. It has a light and thirst-quenching style crested with a bit of dry earthiness and is a good choice for a casual pizza or pasta night. Medium-bodied with 12% alc.

Bit of History
Bardolino wine has been produced in the Veneto region of Italy since the Bronze Age (3300–2000 B.C.E.).

RED

Sebeka Shiraz Pinotage "Cape Blend," Western Cape, South Africa

Pull the leopard-print stopper on this wine and pour yourself a taste of the Cape. Starting with smoked blackberries on the nose, this wine moves swiftly across the palate with sleek, smooth flavors of meat, berries, soil, and spice. This blend of 58% Shiraz and 42% Pinotage is a very good value and a great way to spend a fire-lit evening. Full-bodied with 13.5% alc.

Food Pairing
Chief winemaker of Sebeka Wines, Andries Blake, says the Sebeka Shiraz Pinotage "Cape Blend" is "a perfect companion for duck, roasts, tomato-based pastas, and dark chocolate."

$$$$ RED BLENDS

GOOD

BETTER

Folie à Deux Ménage à Trois Red Table Wine, California, USA

Ménage à Trois is described perfectly by the producers: "On top we've got Zinfandel, a saucy tease that brings blackberry and raspberry jam to the relationship. Merlot, with its generous mouthfeel and red fruits, fits perfectly in the middle. The rich flavors and firm tannins of Cabernet Sauvignon make it the ideal candidate for the bottom layer of the trio." Full-bodied with 13.5% alc.

Penfolds Koonunga Hill Cabernet Merlot, South Eastern Australia

This wine breaks like a wave of unbridled red and black fruit on the nose and palate. But don't let the initial exuberance fool you. Stay with it awhile and see it evolve toward intriguing complexity: earthy, leathery notes peel away to reveal layers of bittersweet chocolate, espresso, tobacco, and flowers. The suede mouthfeel ends with a long, leathery finish. Full-bodied with 13.5% alc.

BEST

Penfolds Koonunga Hill Shiraz Cabernet, South Australia

Dense purple wine with a peppered and smoked berry nose that seems to explode in the mouth with blackberry purée, blackcurrant, plum, rawhide, bonfire, and peppercorn. Marble-smooth and rich with an appealing tannic grip on the finish. A real pleasure to drink. Full-bodied with 13.5% alc.

Exception that Proves the Rule
Generally, big brands under $15 are not made to age, but Penfolds Koonunga Hill Shiraz Cabernet—made from two notably age-worthy grape varieties—will certainly benefit from at least 2, and as many as 10, years of proper cellaring.

RED

95

Escudo Rojo, Baron Philippe de Rothschild, Maipo, Chile

This wine blends the traditional grapes of Bordeaux—Cabernet Sauvignon, Merlot, and Cabernet Franc—grown in sun-drenched Chile, and crafted by French producer Baron Philippe de Rothschild. And so we have a wine that tastes something like a yummy red Bordeaux in a good year—oodles of blackcurrant liqueur and chocolate covered cherries with hint of tobacco and a dash black pepper. Full-bodied with 13.5% alc.

Banfi Col di Sasso Cabernet Sauvignon & Sangiovese, Tuscany, Italy

From one of Italy's most respected producers, Castello Banfi, this wine seriously overdelivers for the price. Compelling aromas and flavors of dry pencil shavings, black forest fruit, earth, fire-roasted meat, minerals, truffle, black currant, and dusty cherries lead to a long black olive finish. Full-bodied with 13% alc.

RED BLENDS $$$$

Fast Fact
Col di Sasso translates to "stony hill," and Castello Banfi's wine by this name is a blend of Cabernet Sauvignon and Sangiovese grapes grown on the rockiest slopes of the Banfi estate in Montalcino, Tuscany.

RED

BEST

Big House "The Lineup" GSM Red Wine, Central Coast, California

Impressive to the point that it could be mistaken for its pricier French inspiration, Châteauneuf-du-Pape, this relatively pale and glossy blend of Grenache, Syrah, and Mourvèdre (GSM) starts with undemonstrative aromas before delivering a huge pleasure dose of black and red fruit, truffle, musk, leather, licorice, and dark peppery flavors. Full-bodied with 13.5% alc.

It's a Fact
The most expensive wine to date is actually a red blend. In February 2007, a bottle of 1945 Château Mouton-Rothschild from Bordeaux fetched $310,700 at Sotheby's auction house. The large bottle was a Jeroboam, which holds the equivalent of four standard bottles. The price paid works out to about $15,535 per glass or $1,534 per sip.

10

Cabernet Sauvignon

Cabernet Sauvignon (pronounced *ka-bur-NAY so-vee-NYON*) always smells and tastes of blackcurrant. Yet it can be one of the most complex wines in the world with flavors of cassis, tobacco, coffee, leather, pencil shavings, green bell pepper, grilled meat, Christmas cake, cedar, brambles, and peppercorn as well.

Sure, Bordeaux started the hype with its top Cabernet Sauvignon–based wines commanding extraordinarily high prices for well over a century. But, top makers from elsewhere are certainly making Cabs comparable to those of Bordeaux. With the whole world now trying to make great Cabernet Sauvignon, consumers never had it so good. The glut pushes prices down and quality up, and today there are more stellar Cabs available than any other wine variety. Though the top ones from prestigious regions and properties still fetch huge prices, the ripple effect creates amazing values for $10, give or take a few bucks. To do justice to this happy fact, this chapter is stuffed with as many good, better, best wines as are warranted, which are quite a few. All of the wines recommended here are seriously underpriced.

Pepperwood Grove Cabernet Sauvignon, California, USA

This wine is a refreshing change if you're looking for a light and quaffable style of Cabernet Sauvignon. You'll taste blackberries, stewed raspberries, fresh basil, and spicy oak with a final dash of vanilla on the finish. Deceivingly full-bodied with 13.5% alc.

Stone Cellars by Beringer Cabernet Sauvignon, California, USA

Here's a fresh and velvety Cabernet Sauvignon with hints of eucalyptus and mint showing through the berry fruit. The firm but ripe tannins tug at the tongue a little bit, making this a solid choice to stand up to meat-based meals. Medium- to full-bodied with 13% alc.

CABERNET SAUVIGNON $$

BEST

RED

Hardy's Stamp of Australia Cabernet Sauvignon, South Eastern Australia

Here's a tightly-knit wine with a warm core of ripe fruit from a trusted producer. Flavors of juicy plum and black cherry are tinged with vanilla, cinnamon, and clove to create an easy thrill in a soft, crowd-pleasing style. Fresh, ripe, and delish. Full-bodied with 13.5% alc.

Fetzer Vineyards Valley Oaks Cabernet Sauvignon, California, USA

This delicious blend of fresh berries, creamy cocoa, warm vanilla, and toasty oak is splendidly crafted with refreshing crispness and subtle grip. Full-bodied with 13.5% alc.

Woodbridge by Robert Mondavi Cabernet Sauvignon, California, USA

This startlingly complex Cab tastes of cassis, dry pencil shavings, red meat, and dried herbs (thyme, bay leaf, and marjoram) with a hint of wood and a dash of black peppercorn on the finish. Although not terribly concentrated, if you're interested in a hugely gulpable food wine at a low price, this is it. Medium- to full-bodied with 13% alc.

CABERNET SAUVIGNON $$

Lindemans Bin 45 Cabernet Sauvignon, Australia

Cassis-scented nose leads to a luscious palate of concentrated mixed berries, milk chocolate, dried plum, warm wood, creamy vanilla, and spice. Velvety-textured wine that finishes with coffee and chocolate. Full-bodied with 13.5% alc.

RED

Leaping Horse Vineyards Cabernet Sauvignon, California, USA

The classic aromas and flavors of cassis and ripe red cherry are edged with red and green bell pepper, warm oak, leather, and a hint of mint. This is good, honest wine with a tight little tannic grip on the finish. Full-bodied wine with 13.5% alc.

[yellow tail] Cabernet Sauvignon, South Eastern Australia

This riot of sweet, ripe fruit is an ideal cocktail wine. Pronounced aromas of blackcurrant liqueur and chocolate lead to succulent flavors of blackberry, cherry, and vanilla cream. This wine would be a hit at a backyard barbecue. Not complex but certainly intense with scrupulously clean, articulate flavors and a satisfyingly smooth mouthfeel. Full-bodied with 13.5% alc.

Black Box Wines Cabernet Sauvignon, California, USA

Who says boxed wine can't be fabulous? If in doubt, taste this. It's a well-made Cab with all the dappled complexity, dry concentration, and long length of its more reputable bottled peers at a fraction of the price. Blackcurrant, cassis, cherry, chocolate, pepper, and a hint of warm wood with a soft grip on the finish mean great value. Full-bodied with 13.5% alc.

RED

CABERNET SAUVIGNON

GOOD

BETTER

Cavit Collection Cabernet Sauvignon , Trentino DOC, Italy

Warm breath of black cherry purée, cassis, lavender, and caramel on the nose. That alone is worth the price. Then, it zips across the palate with simple mixed berries and a hint of green pepper. If you prefer Old World subtlety to New World lushness, this wine's for you. Great food wine with its quenching acidity and restrained style. Medium-bodied with 12.5% alc.

Rosemount Diamond Label Cabernet Sauvignon, South Eastern Australia

Seductive warm berry perfume leads to a dense palate of tightly-coiled black-currant and black cherry flavors. Rich yet crisp, smooth, and full of fruit, but the real value of the wine is its texture: imagine crushed velvet with a fine sheen. Just gorgeous. Full-bodied with 13.5% alc.

**Columbia Crest Two Vines
Cabernet Sauvignon,
Washington State, USA**

Wild blueberries and
smoky oak aromas lead to a
mouth-filling crush of dark
berries with lots of depth
underneath: creamy vanilla,
milk chocolate, coal, coffee, earth, leather, and anise. A suave, sophisticated,
and undervalued wine with
firm but ripe tannins. Full-
bodied with 13.5% alc.

RED

$$$$ CABERNET SAUVIGNON

Beringer Founders' Estate Cabernet Sauvignon, California, USA

This chocolate- and cherry-scented wine is nuanced with cassis, peppercorn, and vanilla. Juicy, ripe extract is underpinned with finely-grained tannins to create proper structure for the fruit. Full-bodied with 13.9% alc.

Concha y Toro Casillero del Diablo Cabernet Sauvignon, Central Valley, Chile

Grilled meat aromas lead to thunderclap flavors of ripe berries, dried currants, cappuccino, chocolate, pipe tobacco, and earth. This wine is quite intense without compromising elegance. Full-bodied with 13.5% alc.

CABERNET SAUVIGNON $$$$

BEST

Rodney Strong Sonoma County Cabernet Sauvignon, California, USA

This wine seems to writhe against the palate, releasing flavors of cassis, leather, medicinal notes, freshly-turned black earth, tobacco, pencil shavings, cigars, spice box, and bitter chocolate. Such great varietal expression and finesse that it could be mistaken for a fine Bordeaux. Rippling fruit pushes up against ripe tannin and firm structure. Serious stuff at a bargain price. Full-bodied with 13.8% alc.

RED

$$$$ CABERNET SAUVIGNON

McWilliam's Hanwood Estate Cabernet Sauvignon, South Eastern Australia

Warm aromas of stewed berries draw you toward a full, fleshy palate of black-currant, plums, and bright cherry edged with floral, leafy notes. Lively and accessible wine with a generous cherry-vanilla finish. Full-bodied with 13.5% alc.

Blackstone Winery Cabernet Sauvignon, California, USA

Quintessential fruit bomb here. An initial blast of berry flavor cascades with rushing notes of cherry, saddle leather, warm caramel, and spice anchored by fine, ripe tannins. The finish is all about cherries and leather. Full-bodied with 13.5% alc.

CABERNET SAUVIGNON **$$$$**

BEST

Clos du Bois North Coast Cabernet Sauvignon, California, USA

Grace yes, but power, too, is dissolved here. This Californian Cabernet wraps the tongue in crushed velvet saturated with flavors of cherry liqueur, blackcurrant purée, bitter black chocolate, fresh coffee, and super-ripe black cherries edged with black pepper. Impeccably balanced with a long and warm vanilla, chocolate, and cassis finish. Great value from a reliable producer. Full-bodied with 13.5% alc.

Decant
Every wine in this chapter would benefit from decanting. To do so, pour the wine into a decanter, glass jug, or clean, empty wine bottle before serving. This allows the wine to open and soften through exposure to air. But once decanted, it doesn't keep well, so drink up.

GOOD

BETTER

J. Lohr Seven Oaks Cabernet Sauvignon, Paso Robles, California, USA

Attractive aromas and flavors of cherry, plum, toast, red licorice, cedar, and the faintest whiff of smoke create exciting complexity in this plush-textured wine with a long vanilla-mocha finish. Full-bodied with 13.5% alc.

Wolf Blass Yellow Label Cabernet Sauvignon, South Australia

This well-loved wine is consistently delicious. Smooth, dark, and luscious plum and black cherry purée flavors are marbled with eucalyptus, mint, and dark chocolate. Succulent, generous, and long with a spicy lick of cigar box and vanilla on the finish. Full-bodied with 13.5% alc.

BEST

It's a Myth
Simply opening a bottle to let it breathe does precious little for the flavor because it only exposes the surface area in the bottleneck to air. If you want to let a wine breathe, decant it or pour it into stemware ahead of time.

RED

Columbia Crest Grand Estates Cabernet Sauvignon, Washington State, USA

This wine is like the best Black Forest cake you've ever eaten: tart cherries, rich chocolate, and cool whipped cream with just a hint of espresso somewhere. The flavors are refined, silky, and precise, finishing with a lingering milk chocolate aftertaste. Full-bodied with 13.5% alc.

ROBERT MONDAVI

PRIVATE SELECTION.

Merlot

CALIFORNIA

11

Merlot

If you like plump, lush cherries dunked in melted chocolate, you will probably like fine Merlot (pronounced *mare-LOW*) because that's essentially what it tastes like. In best cases, it's the smoothest, most supple, and most accessible of all reds.

If Cabernet Sauvignon is power, Merlot is finesse. If Syrah is firm and muscular, Merlot is soft and fleshy. If Pinot Noir is complex and challenging, Merlot is relatively straightforward and opulent. The archetypal thoroughbred—Château Pétrus from Bordeaux—fetches $2,000 to $3,000 per bottle at auction for its opulence. Without question, it is the Merlot against which all others are judged. But you can get serious pleasure from a glass of Merlot for a fraction of the price of Pétrus because, to some degree, Merlot is Merlot—much like vanilla ice cream is vanilla ice cream. And if you buy a good brand like Häagen-Dazs, you're in good shape. This chapter points out the Häagen-Dazses of Merlot.

There's something you should know about this variety, though; cheap Merlot is usually thin, flat, and dire—though the $$ ones recommended here are obviously exceptions. Best to shell out more than $10 for this variety because the wine usually overdelivers at this price point—a fact reflected in the bulging $$$$ category in this chapter. In a nutshell: with Merlot, trade up.

Bella Sera Merlot, Sicily, Italy

Distinct aromas of home-made cherry jam on bread leads to a dry, soft wine reminiscent of cherry-vanilla butter pound cake. Here's a lush, easy-drinking Merlot that's an ideal mid-week quaffer. Full-bodied with 13.5% alc.

Woodbridge by Robert Mondavi Merlot, California, USA

Smooth and balanced with lean aromas and flavors of black cherry, blackberry, cedar, spice, and a light sifting of soft, dark cocoa powder. A mellow mid-week quaffer. Full-bodied with 13.5% alc.

The Little Penguin Merlot, South Eastern Australia

This energetic wine flits from blueberries to leather to strawberries to chocolate. It features plump yet elegant fruit with a velvety texture and intense concentration. This best-value Merlot offers exceptional purity of fruit and a lingering vanilla finish. Full-bodied with 13.5% alc.

RED

[yellow tail] Merlot, South Eastern Australia

Port-like aromas lead to a full-on, off-dry palate of ripe berries and spice. A soft, supple, and lush wine that's an undeniably good value. Full-bodied with 13.5% alc.

Stone Cellars by Beringer Merlot, California, USA

A silky, smooth flow of summer berries daubed with red meat, black cherry jam, and anise with the suggestion of bitter chocolate and coffee on the finish. A soft and approachable wine. Full-bodied with 13% alc.

BEST

Barefoot Merlot, California, USA

Aromas of homemade blueberry pie lead to a dry but berry-rich attack of sun-drenched black and red cherry, wild blueberry, raspberry, and dark chocolate flavors—one fell swoop of satisfaction. An exuberant, very well-made, and quite underpriced wine. Full-bodied with 13.5% alc.

RED

GOOD

BETTER

Fetzer Vineyards Valley Oaks Merlot, California, USA

This pure-fruited Merlot starts with muted berry aromas then slides across the palate with polished cherries and blackberries framed with warm toffee and light herbal notes. A simple, honest value. Full-bodied with 13.5% alc.

Bogle Vineyards Merlot, California, USA

Lots of creamy, toasty vanilla oak underpinning ripe cherry, spicy pipe to-bacco, and melted chocolate on the nose and palate. It has a sleek mouthfeel with a slight tannic grip on the finish. Stylish and full-bodied with 13.5% alc.

BEST

Rosemount Diamond Label Merlot, South Eastern Australia

With freshness and charm, rich aromas of bramble berries and stewed plum lead to a massive hit of velvety ripe fruit and toasty oak flavors. Such succulence! Full-bodied with 13.5% alc.

RED

$$$$ MERLOT

Blackstone Winery Merlot, California, USA

This wine has an air of cowboy country about it— dusty berries, dried leather, warm clove, and smoky wood. It's a smooth and easy Merlot. Full-bodied with 13.5% alc.

Robert Mondavi Private Selection Merlot, California, USA

This jammy Merlot exudes rich aromas of stewed black cherries before sliding across the palate with tightly-knit flavors of black cherry jam, raisins, dark choco-late, dried plum, and Christmas cake. Quite full-bodied wine with 13.5% alc.

MERLOT $$$$

BEST

RED

Concha y Toro Casillero del Diablo Merlot, Rapel Valley, Chile

This wine offers outstanding value. Pronounced aromas of black cherries and coal lead to an incredibly sumptuous and utterly seamless palate. Smooth, rich, mouth-coating flavors of black plum, cedar, and black cherry, as well as a plunging mineral depth that gives the wine quite a grown-up feel. Full-bodied with 13.5% alc.

123

$$$$ MERLOT

GOOD

BETTER

Little Black Dress Merlot, California, USA

Like the classic little black dress made famous by Audrey Hepburn, this wine is a versatile go-to number. It starts with subtle berry aromas before dashing off with saturated flavors of stewed plum, dried cranberry, dark berries, herbs, and a touch of spice from contact with French oak. Full-bodied with 13.5% alc.

Red Truck Central Coast Merlot, California, USA

Cherries poached in sugar on the nose leads to a ripe palate of glazed red berries nuanced with dry cocoa, warm wood, and cracked pepper. A clean, well-made wine. Full-bodied with 13.5% alc.

BEST

J. Lohr Estates Los Osos Merlot, Paso Robles, California, USA

Precise aromas of raspberry jam, cherry, and crushed blueberry lead to a captivatingly complex palate of raspberry jam layered with blackberry, prune, turned earth, damp stones, cedar, tobacco leaf, tar, and sweet spice. A plush and lustrous texture pervades this full-bodied wine with 13.5% alc.

History
Merlot was brought to California in the mid-nineteenth century and is now one of the leading red wines uncorked in the United States. Americans drank 26.8 million cases of Merlot in 2008—a huge increase from 2.8 million cases in 1994.

Food Pairing
The winemaker for J. Lohr's Los Osos Merlot, Jeff Meier, recommends pairing the wine with roasted beef or lamb with a berry-based reduction sauce.

Murphy-Goode Alexander Valley Merlot, California, USA

Unlike most Merlots, this wine is a serious blockbuster. Dried cherry aromas lead to a powerful and concentrated attack of dried cherries, stewed blackberries, and bay leaf. It offers a thoroughly mouth-coating experience, and the texture is like silk. If you like intense wines, you'll love this full-bodied Californian with 13.5% alc.

Rodney Strong Sonoma County Merlot, California, USA

Such solid value! Ripe cherries and blueberries on the nose lead to cherries, plums, blueberries, creamy vanilla, and toasted spice on the palate. Exactly what a great Merlot should taste like with superb concentration, complexity, and length. Full-bodied with 13.8% alc.

BEST

Columbia Crest Grand Estates Merlot, Columbia Valley, Washington State, USA

Warm chocolate cake and blackberry aromas lead to an opulent palate of dried plum, black and red berries, and again chocolate cake—with a chocolate mousse mouthfeel. This is an incredibly tightly-knit wine with an artisanal, "crafted" not "produced," air about it. Serious wine at an unbelievably low price. Full-bodied with 13.5% alc.

GOOD

BETTER

Beringer Founders' Estate Merlot, California, USA

This refreshing and approachable wine brims with aromas and flavors of homemade cherry pie, fresh blackberries, and tart boysenberries edged with a hint of spearmint. Quite a crisp version of this varietal. Pleasant, full-bodied wine with 13.9% alc.

Sonoma Vineyards Merlot, Sonoma County, California, USA

A flash of sweet-talking fruit broadens quickly to reveal real depth and brilliance. Bold blackberry, plum, chocolate, and violet flavors are shot through with tart red cherry. Full-bodied with 13.8% alc.

BEST

Columbia Crest H3 Horse Heaven Hills Merlot, Washington State, USA

Supremely silken palate of super-ripe berries drenched in the creamiest milk chocolate ever. Fabulous texture that feels smooth, cool, and polished to a high gloss. Utterly delicious. Full-bodied with 14.1% alc.

RED

the Little Penguin™

SOUTH EASTERN AUSTRALIA
SHIRAZ

VINTAGE
2003

750ml

13.5% alc./vol.
RED WINE
VIN ROUGE

PRODUCT OF AUSTRALIA / PRODUIT D'AUSTRALIE

12

Syrah/Shiraz

Syrah (pronounced *see-RAH*) is a tightly-wound wine that tastes of blackberries, blueberries, meat, black pepper, and smoke. Shiraz (pronounced *shir-AHZ*), the Australian version of the same grape, is less spicy with a slightly sweeter, riper, dark chocolate character.

The most important thing to know about Syrah/Shiraz is that it usually delivers the best value of any grape variety at the lower price points—especially when it comes from Australia. The more premium Aussie Shirazes are stealing the show from France's Rhône Syrahs revered for centuries. No, your average Aussie Shiraz won't always deliver the same subtlety and restraint as a Rhône Syrah, and you don't get much of the savory quality found in the French stuff, but the Australian sunshine-in-a-glass version also tastes great. Furthermore, it's bottled ready to drink, generally costs less, and is usually easier to find because of wide distribution and large production volumes. In short, Australian Shiraz is a godsend to wine lovers.

Areas of California, Washington, Argentina, Chile, and elsewhere also toy with this grape variety, usually calling it Shiraz when it's made in the Aussie style and Syrah if it's more Rhône-like. And much of it is inspiringly good value. That's what this chapter is all about: revealing riveting Shiraz and Syrah at reasonable prices.

Pepperwood Grove Syrah, California, USA

Sweet wild blueberry aromas lead to flavors reminiscent of bumbleberry pie—quite jammy with a hint of earthiness and vanilla. Full-bodied with 13.5% alc.

[yellow tail] Shiraz, South Eastern Australia

The nose needs a little coaxing but the palate is a vibrant hit of blueberries, raspberries, and spice. This wine is one big swirl of happy juice, with tons of sweet ripe fruit balanced with a tad of appealing earthiness on the finish. Full-bodied with 13.5% alc.

Barefoot Shiraz, California, USA

The winemaker's notes read, "This wine will have you at hello," and she's right—it's immediately captivating. It swells with blackberry jam and stewed plums before arcing and tapering to smoke, peppercorn, and lavender. All this is followed by the richest, creamiest mocha ever resonating on the finish. Gorgeous mouthfeel—silky but structured. Full-bodied with 13.5% alc.

RED

Hardy's Stamp of Australia Shiraz, South Eastern Australia

This is an easy, approachable wine with mouthfilling flavors of dark chocolate, dried plums, and juicy raspberries as well as hints of oven-fresh bread and white pepper. Full-bodied with 13.5% alc.

The Little Penguin Shiraz, South Eastern Australia

Port-like richness on the nose leads to an incredibly compact palate of boysenberry compote, fresh blackberries, black cherries, and plum jam. Loads of aromatic, sweet fruit feels soft and hefty in the mouth, is anchored with firm structure, and finishes with a spicy little kick of white pepper. Full-bodied with 13.5% alc.

BEST

Jacob's Creek Shiraz, South Australia

Explosive flavors and aromas of black plum purée, blackberry, earth, jam, charcoal, and peppercorn flood the senses. This is a robust and untamed blockbuster with no hard edges and a lush mouthfeel. It's so dense you could almost spoon this wine into your mouth. Full-bodied with 14% alc.

GOOD

BETTER

Hardy's Nottage Hill Shiraz, South Eastern Australia

Here's quite a spicy Shiraz with flavors and aromas of blackberry, black cherry, clove, and black pepper. It's a bit leaner than most Shirazes with a peppered warmth on the finish. Medium- to full-bodied with 13% alc.

Lindemans Bin 50 Shiraz, Australia

Muted aromas of sun-warmed berries lead to exuberant flavors of stewed black forest fruit shot through with taut acidity. Bright, fresh, and fleshy with hints of smoke and pepper. Long, dark chocolate finish. Full-bodied with 13.5% alc.

Black Box Wines Central Coast Shiraz, Central Coast, California, USA

With smooth, concentrated black cherry and black-currant flavors laced with cindery smoke and spice, a long, peppered finish, and a satisfying grip of ripe tannin, this wine will almost certainly challenge your assumptions about bag-in-box wine. It's solid proof that outstanding value can indeed come in a carton. Full-bodied with 13.5% alc.

RED

GOOD

BETTER

Black Swan Shiraz, South Eastern Australia

Black Swan Shiraz offers a bright, clean lick of cherry-vanilla with notes of charcoal, black peppercorn, damp clay, and milk chocolate. Well-balanced with a long, creamy finish. Full-bodied with 13.5% alc.

Rosemount Diamond Label Shiraz, South Eastern Australia

This opaque wine starts with muted berry aromas before sliding across the palate all lush and decadent, unfurling focused layers of plum jam, blackberries, cassis, plum pudding, lingering oak, and a final hit of bitter chocolate. This quintessential Aussie Shiraz is warm and generous, long and resonating. Full-bodied with 13.5% alc.

SYRAH/SHIRAZ $$$

Trapiche Oak Cask Syrah, Mendoza, Argentina

This deeply-colored—almost black—wine starts with an intoxicating aroma of a wood-burning fire and cherries. Next, seriously mouth-filling flavors of red and black cherries hit the palate, imbued with steady notes of warm wood and smoke. Grippy tannins hold the wine in place, giving it a certain gravitas, and a long, spicy, black pepper finish punctuates it. Very full-bodied with 14% alc.

History Lesson
Though there are many theories as to this variety's origins, DNA testing confirmed in 1998 that Syrah originated in France's northern Rhône region and may have been around since A.D. 77.

Oak Influence
American and French oak impart different flavors to a wine. American oak generally adds vanilla, butterscotch, and coconut notes while French oak tends to add nuttiness and spiciness. French oak also tends to smooth a wine's texture more so than American oak.

RED

$$$$ SYRAH/SHIRAZ

Red Knot of Australia Shiraz, McLaren Vale, South Australia

The rather knotty closure—a red pull-tab of spiraled plastic leading to the bulbous end—is amusingly phallic. And, the closure's official tagline is "Easier to get off." I kid you not. But once you get past that and taste it, you'll find appealing aromas and flavors of ripe mixed berries, black cherry liqueur, tobacco, dried flowers, chocolate, lime oil, and orange rind. Full-bodied with 14% alc.

J. Lohr Estates South Ridge Syrah, Paso Robles, California, USA

Quiet scents of summer berries on the nose lead to long, reflective flavors of strawberry jam, boysenberry, green olive, fresh fig, orange peel, cherry, and spice. Eighteen months in French and American oak is felt as warm complexity permeating the plump, plush fruit. Full-bodied with 13.5% alc.

SYRAH/SHIRAZ $$$$

Hess Syrah, Mendocino and Monterey Counties, California, USA

With a rich garnet hue, this revved-up wine is a brisk blast of concentrated blackberry, blueberry, white pepper, and black cherry flavors that roars along all dense, dry, and smooth with an incredible crushed velvet texture and a deep charred wood and toffee finish. Tannins are round and ripe with some grip and a bright, tart seam of acidity. Seriously full-bodied with 14.5% alc.

Knotty Talk

Red Knot of Australia Shiraz is one of the first wines sealed under Zork, an environmentally-friendly closure that seals like a screw cap, pops like a cork, and can be easily reinserted back into the bottle.

Food Pairing

The winemaker for J. Lohr Estates South Ridge Syrah, Jeff Meier, recommends pairing the wine with hearty braised meats or a savory tri-tip with an ancho chile glaze.

RED

It's a Hit!

In the early part of the twenty-first century, Syrah/Shiraz became one of the top 10 most widely planted wine grapes in the world.

Penfolds Koonunga Hill Shiraz, South Australia

This textbook Aussie Shiraz offers intense poached plum and stewed forest fruits on the nose and palate laced with a touch of milk chocolate and white pepper. It's a soft, mouthcoating, good-quality wine. Full-bodied with 13.5% alc.

Bonterra Vineyards Syrah, Mendocino County, California, USA

This Syrah is mixed with dashes of Grenache and Viognier in the Rhône tradition, which softens the Syrah and adds juiciness and complexity. Tightly-coiled flavors of crushed wild blueberry, bright cherry, grilled meat, chalky gravel, cola, and spice imbue this solid Californian Syrah. Great match for grilled beef. Very full-bodied with 15% alc.

BEST

Columbia Crest Grand Estates Shiraz, Washington State, USA

This opaque wine starts with a whiff of fresh rare beef and blueberries before erupting on the palate with flavors of blueberry, dark chocolate, black coffee, violet, and black pepper over a tight mineral core. A fine web of bright and refreshing acidity adds structure to the dark fruit. Then, on the finish, a note of warm dark chocolate coats the palate. Full-bodied with 13.5% alc.

Serving Temperature
Syrah/Shiraz is best served close to room temperature—about 65°F.

RED

143

$$$$ SYRAH/SHIRAZ

Jacob's Creek Reserve Shiraz, South Australia

Expect an explosion of flavor. This seriously concentrated Shiraz blasts the taste buds with full-throttle black and red cherries, vanilla, and black pepper. Not hugely complex but extreme concentration and length here. Very full-bodied with 14% alc.

Toasted Head Dunnigan Hills Shiraz, California, USA

This wine brims with generous flavors of cranberry, raspberry, plum, cedar, and lavender. Twelve months in American oak softens the edges and adds a note of warm vanilla. It's an engaging drink with a nice balance of dark fruit and sassy spirit. Full-bodied with 13.5% alc.

Concha y Toro Casillero del Diablo Syrah, Rapel Valley, Chile

There are all kinds of hidden depths here. Pure poached blackberry fruit on the nose leads to a savory palate of smoked bacon, wet pebbles, sage, cocoa, and cream. Compact flavors, bright acidity, and ripe tannins add structure to this smooth, long, and deeply undervalued wine. Full-bodied with 13.5% alc.

RED

BERINGER

THIRD CENTURY

III

CENTRAL COAST
PINOT NOIR

SINCE 1876

B

13

Pinot Noir

Pinot Noir (pronounced *pee-no NWAHR*) tastes of canned strawberry, cooked cranberry, and violet. After a while in the bottle, it shifts toward flavors of beets, underbrush, and barnyard (which can actually be quite intriguing as a subtle nuance in a wine giving it earthy almost primal appeal, perhaps comparable to smelly cheese).

Pinot Noir is a relatively light, smooth, refreshing red wine that can be incredibly complex and beguiling. In fact, before the 2004 flick *Sideways*, Pinot-philes were like a secret sect of hardcore oenophiles sharing their private passion for this variety, which can make silky wines of drop-dead elegance—seriously seductive stuff. Then *Sideways* blew the club wide open. Almost everyone who saw the film flocked to taste this holy grail of red wine. Winemakers in California, referring to the "*Sideways* effect," responded swiftly by cutting Merlot vines off at the trunk and grafting on Pinot Noir.

Now, everyone wants in on the game and winemakers are churning out Pinot Noir everywhere from the United States to Australia. As they toil away in the vineyards and wineries to capture the elusive thrill factor of Pinot Noir, some very good versions are hitting shelves at much more affordable prices than those fine caliber—but very expensive—gems from the variety's heartland of Burgundy, France. To see what I mean, just taste through some of the wines recommended in this chapter.

Citra Pinot Noir, Puglia, Italy

This wine starts with the merest suggestion of wild rose on the nose before invigorating the palate with tart ripe raspberry and canned strawberry flavors that evolve toward a beet-root earthiness. It's a classic Pinot Noir that's clean and well-made. Medium- to full-bodied with 13% alc.

Bella Sera Pinot Noir, Provincia di Pavia, Italy

A black plum and raspberry jam nose leads to an elegant palate of stewed strawberries, ripe raspberries, minerals, and a gentle shake of black pepper. Medium-bodied with 12.5% alc.

PINOT NOIR   **$$**

Nutritional Information
The average 5-oz. glass of Pinot Noir contains 121 calories and 3.4 g carbohydrates.

BEST

Turning Leaf Pinot Noir, Pfalz, Germany

This wine shows a muted nose of ripe berries followed by a strawberry-rich attack that's clean and crisp, bright and balanced. With perky simplicity and a slightly peppered finish, this delightfully approachable wine delivers excellent value for the price. Medium-bodied with 12.5% alc.

The *Sideways* Effect
Right after the release of the hit movie *Sideways*, U.S. supermarket sales of Pinot Noir skyrocketed. The movie was released on October 22, 2004. Between October 24, 2004, and July 2, 2005, supermarket sales of this variety jumped 18 percent over the same period a year earlier.

RED

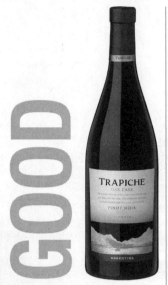

Trapiche Oak Cask Pinot Noir, Mendoza, Argentina

Flavors and aromas of raspberry jam on toast, vanilla cream, warm oak, and sweet tobacco swirl around in this bold style of Pinot Noir with a very peppery finish. Full-bodied with 13.5% alc.

Cavit Collection Pinot Noir, Provincia di Pavia IGT, Italy

This is a light, captivating wine with wafting aromas of homemade strawberry jam that lead to bright fresh strawberry flavors edged with delicate floral notes of lavender and violet. A core of wet stones give this Italian Pinot Noir exciting mineral depth, and the black olive finish suggests it would fare well with food. Medium-bodied with 12% alc.

BEST

Mark West Pinot Noir, Sonoma County, California, USA

What a delicious wine! Aromatic flavors of raspberries, violets, vanilla, and clove characterize this richly-fruited, seductive Pinot Noir with resonating length. Along with considerable concentration, this wine is silky yet well-structured with taut acidity and soft, supple tannins. Such finesse! Full-bodied with 13.8% alc.

History

Pinot Noir is ancient. It was known to the Romans in 100 A.D. and cultivated in Burgundy, France, as early as the fourth century A.D.

It's a Fact

Mark West is one of the top five best-selling Pinot Noirs under $15 in the United States.

RED

151

Jacob's Creek Reserve Pinot Noir, South Eastern Australia

This Pinot Noir brims with aromas and flavors of peppered raspberry jam. Clean and well made with a firm little grip on the finish. Full-bodied with 13.5% alc.

Robert Mondavi Private Selection Pinot Noir, California, USA

This wine is textbook Pinot Noir. Tinned strawberries on the nose and palate followed by flavors of dark beetroot and tree bark laced with damp herbs. It has a silky smooth mouthfeel and a refreshing zip of acidity. Full-bodied with 13.5% alc.

PINOT NOIR $$$$

Food Pairing
Pinot Noir is a perfect match for grilled salmon or roasted poultry, lamb, or ham.

BEST

Beringer Third Century Pinot Noir, Central Coast, California, USA

Lush nose of super-ripe raspberries leads to a ripe raspberry jam palate that evolves toward flavors of violet, beetroot, and earthy woodlands resonating on the finish. Pinot Noir lovers will appreciate the subtle nod to this noble varietal's heartland— Burgundy. Full-bodied with 13.9% alc.

It's a Fact
Pinot Noir is the world's most challenging vine variety with which to make wine. It mutates easily, is susceptible to disease, and yields thin, pale, acerbic wine if the winemaker isn't very careful or the vines are grown in unsuitable places. This means it's high risk for winemakers and drinkers alike.

RED

GOOD

BETTER

Red Truck California Pinot Noir, California, USA

Attractive fresh strawberry and cherry aromas lead to a clean, fresh-tasting wine with crisp cranberry, red plum, and strawberry flavors. An uncomplicated and versatile food wine. Medium-bodied with 13% alc.

Concannon Limited Release Pinot Noir, Central Coast, California, USA

This charming Pinot Noir exudes classic strawberry, beetroot, and earth aromas before slipping toward silky flavors of cherries, strawberries, beets, and an appealing wet stone minerality. Medium-bodied with 13% alc.

PINOT NOIR $$$$

BEST

Bogle Vineyards Pinot Noir, Russian River Valley, California, USA

Incredible nose! Oven-fresh cherry cake and cool vanilla cream lead to a seductive palate of the same with a hint of white pepper on the finish. Not complex but incredibly well-made, silken, refined, and long. Full-bodied with 14.2% alc.

What's It Worth?
Pinot Noir is a grape full of promise, and no one delivers on that promise like Romanée-Conti, the revered Burgundy against which all other Pinot Noir is judged. NYwines/Christie's in New York sold six magnums of the 1985 vintage at auction for $170,375 in March 2006. A single magnum holds the equivalent of two regular-size bottles so this wine cost roughly $14,198 per 750 ml, $2,840 per glass, and $284 per sip.

RED

14

Zinfandel

Zinfandel (pronounced *ZIN-fan-dell*) tastes of ripe, juicy blackberries and raspberries edged with black pepper. It's a rich, firmly-structured wine with deep color, full body, and high alcohol.

Zinfandel is to America as Shiraz is to Australia—the nation's flagship red variety. And in California, Zinfandel found its niche. Not only are the growing conditions ideal for this grape but the wine suits American cuisine perfectly. The massive weight and peppery richness match everything from casual burgers and chili to barbecued ribs and steak.

Although Zinfandel can make fabulous wines of deep concentration, considerable complexity, and mighty power, quality does vary dramatically. The big reason is that, unlike many other wine grapes, Zinfandel tends to ripen quite unevenly, producing harsh, green berries on the same bunch as super-ripe ones that raisin quickly if left unpicked. But some producers still manage to produce stellar, gorgeously ripe Zinfandel that's dry, sturdy, and seriously fun to drink.

This chapter reveals some of the best big-brand Zinfandels on the market.

CK Mondavi Family Vineyards Wildcreek Canyon Zinfandel, California, USA

Brimming with fresh raspberries, this wine is a bit more tart than most Zins yet it is quite refreshing and well-balanced with warm vanilla and spicy black pepper on the finish. Full-bodied with 13.9% alc.

Pepperwood Grove Old Vine Zinfandel, California, USA

Smoked meat aromas lead to rich flavors of cherries, beef, and poached black forest fruits before finishing with a slick of toasty oak and spice. Fruity and full-bodied with 13.5% alc.

ZINFANDEL $$

Nutritional Information
The average 5-oz. glass of Zinfandel contains 129 calories and 4.2 g carbohydrates.

BEST

Barefoot Zinfandel, Lodi, California, USA

A standout value with loads of rich, spicy black fruits, smooth, creamy vanilla, and a sumptuous mouth-feel. Seriously impressive wine for the price. Make it your go-to Zin. Full-bodied with 13.5% alc.

Did You Know
Zinfandel was first planted in California at the time of the Gold Rush, around 1855. Today, about 52,000 acres of Zinfandel vines populate California, making it the third most widely-planted wine grape in the state.

RED

Ravenswood Vintners Blend Zinfandel, California, USA

Ravenswood specializes in Zinfandel, and you can tell. This wine is a reliable mouthful of super-ripe berries, dried earth, pepper, cinnamon, and mocha. Bright acidity and a bit of grip on the finish lend structure to the sweet fruit. Full-bodied with 13.5% alc.

Twisted Old Vine Zinfandel, California, USA

Kick back, twist the cap, and indulge in this under-priced wine that starts with a creamy note of nutmeg on the nose before saturating the palate with concentrated flavors of black cherry, blueberry, blackberry jam, black pepper, and melting dark chocolate. An exciting medley of tight flavors is wound up in this firmly-structured, full-bodied wine with 14% alc.

BEST

RED

**Bogle Vineyards Old Vine
Zinfandel, California, USA**

This hulking but well-
defined and fairly serious
wine made from 40- to
80-year-old vines is loaded
with raspberry jam, blackberry jam, wild blueberry,
black cherry, black pepper,
tobacco, clove, smoke,
and oak with a long, warm
wood finish. The bold
fruit is wrapped around a
muscular frame. Very full-
bodied with 14.8% alc.

$$$$ ZINFANDEL

**J. Lohr Estates Old Vines
Zinfandel, Paso Robles,
California, USA**

With flavors and aromas of
raspberry jam and mixed
fresh berries edged with
black pepper, black licorice,
and black tea, this wine offers great value. Very full-
bodied with 14.9% alc.

**Murphy-Goode Zinfandel
Liar's Dice, Sonoma County,
California, USA**

Tightly-packed flavors
and aromas of black
bramble fruits—black
raspberry, blackcurrant,
and blackberry—are
edged with black pepper
and an appealing earthy
minerality. Much of the
fruit is sourced from old
vines, contributing to the
intense concentration of
this wine. Very full-bodied
with 14.9% alc. This Zin
benefits from double
decanting.

BEST

Dancing Bull Zinfandel, California, USA

Black cherries and cream on the nose lead to rich and lively flavors of black cherry and peppercorn layered with notes of raspberry, chocolate, café latte, and vanilla. Satin texture, jammy ripeness, electric acidity, and a nice grip on the finish. Full-bodied with 13.9% alc.

Food Pairing

The winemaker for J. Lohr Estates Old Vines Zinfandel, Jeff Meier, recommends pairing Old Vines Zinfandel with casual fare such as grilled sausage with red peppers, zesty red-sauced pasta dishes, or even pizza.

Food Pairing

The makers of Murphy-Goode Liar's Dice say the wine is perfect for backyard barbecues and is best served with lip-smacking baby-back ribs, pulled pork sandwiches, burgers, or anything that combines sweet and spicy flavors.

Double Decanting

To double decant, pour a wine into a decanter or other vessel then right straight back into the original bottle. No need to pause between pours. This double decant offers twice the aerating effect as a single one, and is great for opening up really tight reds such as the Murphy-Goode Zinfandel Liar's Dice.

15

Other Great Reds

Cabernet Sauvignon, Merlot, Shiraz/Syrah, Pinot Noir, and Zinfandel. You know them. You love them. And these varietals account for most of the wines made and drunk in America, so they each deserve an entire chapter in this book. But they don't tell the whole story.

Hundreds of wine grapes exist beyond this small circle, some of which enjoy a certain level of well-deserved popularity in the United States. Quite frankly, this book would be remiss to exclude the tightly-knit Malbecs of Argentina, the bell pepper–scented Carmeneres of Chile, and the cherry-flavored wines of Chianti, just to name a few. Many of these wines could command two times—and maybe even three or four times—their prices if their grape varieties were more prestigious.

This chapter tips a hat to the best of wines beyond the famous five.

Bella Sera Chianti DOCG, Tuscany, Italy

Tumbling flavors and aromas of cherry, raspberry, earth, sea salt, and white pepper characterize this classic, honest-value wine that could grace almost any dinner table. Medium-bodied with 12.5% alc.

Citra Montepulciano d'Abruzzo DOC, Abruzzo, Italy

Such great value! Lush aromas of berries and plum lead to sweet-fruited black cherry and leather flavors with a soft, silky texture and fresh, palate-cleansing acidity. This stellar food wine finishes with peppercorn and a slightly bitter black olive note. Medium- to full-bodied with 13% alc.

BEST

Trapiche Varietals Malbec, Mendoza, Argentina

This wine smells and tastes of fresh plums, blackberries, vanilla, and peppercorn. Sweet, fresh, and full in the mouth with firm, ripe tannins that create a lush velvety texture. It's a seriously underpriced wine with a grown-up feel about it. Full-bodied with 13.5% alc.

Chianti

Made from Sangiovese grapes, Chianti (pronounced *key-ANN-tee*) tends to taste of dusty cherries but can often fan out with notes of flowers, cinnamon, earth, and leather, too.

Montepulciano d'Abruzzo

Montepulciano d'Abruzzo (pronounced *mon-teh-pool-CHAH-no dah-BROOT-so*) is the name of the grape variety and the wine style from the Abruzzo region of Italy. The wine is a simple, unpretentious quaff with deep color and generous, juicy, soft berry flavors. Best not to confuse this wine with Vino Nobile di Montepulciano, a more premium Tuscan wine that tastes totally different because it's made from different grapes.

Malbec

Malbec (pronounced *MAL-beck*) is a dense, inky-dark wine brimming with flavors and aromas of blackberry and dark plum with a smooth but firm structure. It is the flagship red variety of Argentina.

RED

$$$ OTHER GREAT REDS

Gabbiano Chianti DOCG, Tuscany, Italy

This Chianti starts with wafting aromas of beef, cherries, earth, and minerals before caressing the palate with warm and enticing flavors of aged steak cooked rare, dusty cherries, and slight note of green olive. A hint of tannic astringency on the finish reveals a structure that would benefit from food. This is a good value midweek pizza wine. Medium- to full-bodied with 13% alc.

Feudo Arancio Nero d'Avola, Sicily, Italy

This number one selling Nero d'Avola in the United States starts with a sweet caramel apple aroma then zips along with flavors of dark toffee, sweet tobacco, red apple, ripe plum, and black pepper. It's a casual Italian charmer with an air of Old World restraint rather than New World fruit-juiciness—or fruit-*forward*ness as they say in wine circles. It tastes very dry and is quite food friendly. Full-bodied with 13.5% alc.

BEST

Nero d'Avola

Nero d'Avola (pronounced *NEH-roe DAH-voe-lah*), which is the name of both the grape and the wine, tends to be deeply colored and drenched with flavors and aromas of plum and peppercorn. It is Sicily's most popular grape variety and shares a similar taste and texture to Syrah or Shiraz.

Bogle Vineyards Petite Sirah, California, USA

Full-throttle aromas and flavors of super-ripe cherries, butter pound cake, and vanilla custard. The fleshy, ripe, and fantastically expansive texture builds on the palate before finishing with drizzled flavors of melted milk chocolate. It's just a gorgeous wine—the kind that ruins it for the rest with its unabashed hedonistic appeal. This wine could sell for three or four times the price. Full-bodied with 13.5% alc.

Riunite Lambrusco IGT, Emilia, Italy

One mouthful of this and you're back to a time when the punch bowl was the centerpiece of the party. This wine bears an uncanny resemblance to the ubiquitous homemade fruit punch of the '70s and '80s, right down to the slight berry-rich sweetness and gentle effervescence. Easy, soft, nostalgic wine that beats a wine cooler any day. Perfect choice for a picnic. Very light-bodied with just 8% alc.

Trapiche Oak Cask Malbec, Mendoza, Argentina

This outstanding Malbec is a definite crowd-pleaser. It starts with a nose of warm wood and sour cherry before revealing a bright attack of red plum and black cherry flavors edged with tobacco, tar, and char. Full-bodied with 13.5% alc.

BEST

J. Lohr Estates Wildflower Valdiguié, Monterey County, California, USA

Distinct cranberry aromas lead to a crisp palate of strawberry-rhubarb pie and stewed cranberries. It's clean, balanced, and light with great purity of fruit. In fact, this wine is very similar to good Beaujolais and would likewise be a great match for roasted turkey, chicken, or goose. Medium-bodied with 12.5% alc.

Lambrusco
Throughout the 1970s and 1980s, Lambrusco (pronounced *lam-BROO-skoe*) was the biggest-selling import wine in the United States. Lambrusco wine—made from a grape of the same name—is light in body and alcohol, fairly sweet, slightly sparkling, and refreshes with flavors of red grapes, mixed berries, and sometimes an attractive note of violet.

Food Pairing
The winemaker for J. Lohr Estates Wildflower Valdiguié recommends pairing the wine with grilled salmon.

Valdiguié
Pronounced *val-de-GUAY*, this winegrape makes a fruity wine that's relatively light in body and alcohol, tasting of ripe, fresh berries. It's soft and easy-drinking with low tannins and crisp acidity.

RED

Ruffino Chianti DOCG, Tuscany, Italy

This is a beautifully-made, reasonably-priced Chianti of considerable charm. Enticing aromas of violet and cherries lead to wild cherry, earth, pepper, and hazelnuts on the palate. It's medium-bodied and crisp making it a great match for pasta with tomato sauce. 12% alc.

Ravenswood Vintners Blend Petite Sirah, California, USA

Pronounced aromas of black cherries erupt on the palate with tight, smooth flavors of black forest fruits, dark chocolate, leather, subtle nutmeg, and peppercorn. Expect a velvety texture with a firm structure. Full-bodied with 13.5% alc.

Petite Sirah

Petite Sirah (pronounced *pe-TEET see-RAH*) makes a rich wine laden with dark berry fruit and black peppercorn. It is, in fact, a cross between Syrah and the minor Rhône grape, Peloursin. Petite Sirah is darker in color and firmer in structure than Syrah or Shiraz.

RED

Catena Alamos Malbec, Mendoza, Argentina

Here is a brilliant version of Malbec at an incredible price. With dense notes of plum purée, black licorice, black pepper, tar, leather, and roses on the nose and palate, it is complex and smooth with firm, ripe tannins on the finish. Served with grilled meat, it's hard to beat. Full-bodied with 13.5% alc.

GOOD

BETTER

Concannon Limited Release Petite Sirah, Central Coast, California, USA

This interesting wine flits from black cherry to red plum, cocoa to mocha, white pepper to clove. A bright seam of mouth-watering acidity and firm grip of tannin seem to anchor the bold and complex fruit, yielding a rather serious-tasting wine. Full-bodied with 13.5% alc.

Concha y Toro Casillero del Diablo Carmenere, Rapel Valley, Chile

With invigorating flavors and aromas of freshly-cut green peppers, mixed berries, and ripe juicy plums, nuanced with cigar, bitter chocolate, vanilla, and coffee, this is textbook perfect Carmenere with impeccable balance. Elegant, fine tannins give structure to the sweet fruit. I particularly like the long mocha finish. Full-bodied with 13.5% alc.

Carmenere

Though originally from Bordeaux where it was used to add color to the red wines of the Médoc, Carmenere (pronounced *car-men-AIR*) is now the flagship winegrape of Chile. In Chile, Carmenere produces a deeply ruby-colored wine with cherry-plum flavor nuanced with green pepper and sometimes notes of chocolate and violet.

RED

Concha y Toro Casillero del Diablo Malbec, Rapel Valley, Chile

This magnificent value starts with an unmistakable aroma of freshly brewed coffee spiked with Bailey's Irish Cream before striking the palate with exuberant yet seductive flavors of sweet black cherries, coffee, fresh cream, milk chocolate, warm vanilla, and peppercorn. Complexity, succulent fruit, and long length at a reasonable price amounts to stellar value. Full-bodied with 13.5% alc.

$$$$ OTHER GREAT REDS

Louis Jadot Beaujolais-Villages AC, Burgundy, France

This wine packs all the fun of the fair. Wafting aromas of fresh strawberries and candy floss lead to refreshing wild strawberry, ripe raspberry, and red apple flavors. Bright, fruity, easy wine that's made to quaff and quench rather than sip and ponder. Medium-bodied with 12.5% alc.

Don Miguel Gascón Malbec, Mendoza, Argentina

This bold blockbuster is one big heave of stewed blackberries, wild blueberries, and dried plums tinged with espresso and dark chocolate. A final crank of peppercorn on the finish confirms this wine would be a great match for fire-grilled t-bone. Full-bodied with 13.9% alc.

Beaujolais
Made from the Gamay grape, Beaujolais (pronounced *bow-jhuh-LAY*) is a spirited mouthful of strawberry and raspberry fruit. Rarely complex but usually quite fresh and clean-tasting, this wine is one of the few reds best served well-chilled to play up its fruity, quenching character. And because of how it's made, it starts to decline relatively quickly after bottling, so always select the most recent vintage on the shelf.

Trapiche Broquel Malbec, Mendoza, Argentina

Shining purple-black in the glass and suggesting oil-like density, this voluptuous wine exudes pronounced aromas of grilled beef, creamy mocha, and the slightest hint of dry licorice root before sliding across the palate with intense flavors of black and red berries, flame-grilled beef, bitter chocolate, espresso, and dry earth. Brambly fruit stays on the finish for what seems like days. A gratifying wine. Full-bodied with 14% alc.

Rosé and Sparkling Wines

Big House Pink

2007 CALIFORNIA PINK WINE

ALC. 13.0% BY VOL.

16

Rosé

Scantily clad French folk quaff it on beaches of the Côte d'Azur. Euro-version "it" girls sip it in the stylish tapas bars of Spain. And fashionistas enjoy it in beachside eateries from Malibu to Miami. Frankly, in places where rosé is de rigueur, the wine is drank rather than discussed because focus lies elsewhere—on tanned skin, on the view of the ocean, on easy afternoon chit chat—and the wet stuff in the glass merely lubricates and amplifies the experience.

The coral wines of the Côtes de Provence, the magenta *rosados* of Spain, and the salmon White Zinfandels of California are loved locally. And in these and other major markets, rosé consumption is soaring. In France, it even overtook white wine recently in terms of sales volumes for the first time. Pink is huge. Clearly, drinking rosé is no longer something to blush about.

Since there are relatively few pink wines sold in this country over $11, the ultra-premium $$$$ category has been nixed in this chapter. Isn't it nice to know you never have to spend much to get a delicious glass of rosé?

Here's to pink wine!

CK Mondavi Family Vineyards Willow Springs White Zinfandel, California, USA

This bright coral-colored wine with tartly-sweet flavors and aromas of strawberry-rhubarb and candied lemon is zesty, quenching, and easy. Light-bodied with 9.1% alc.

Barefoot White Zinfandel, California, USA

Shatteringly fresh like a summer rainfall, this pinky-orange wine with a slight spritz and sweet watermelon aromas washes over the tongue with flavors of rosewater, sweet pineapple, fresh orange, ripe pear, and cantaloupe. Quite refined for a White Zinfandel. Off-dry and light-bodied with 9.5% alc.

**Beringer California
Collection White Zinfandel,
California, USA**

This coral-rose colored
wine with aromas of strawberry and peach attacks the
palate with a soft shock of
ripe berries and stone fruit.
It is bright, concentrated,
and off-dry with a tart
seam of acidity, making it
an excellent thirst quencher. Light-bodied and juicy
with 10% alc.

**How to Make Pink
Wines**
Pink wines are made by
allowing the color-laden
skins of red grapes to
remain with the juice
briefly—after the fruit is
crushed—to impart extra
flavor, aroma, and color
to the wine. Occasionally,
though, it's made by
mixing red wine with
white, but this method
tends to make an inferior
drink.

ROSÉ/SPARKLING

GOOD

BETTER

Le Rosé de Mouton Cadet, Baron Philippe de Rothschild, Bordeaux Rosé AC, Bordeaux, France

This pale blend of Merlot, Cabernet Franc, and Cabernet Sauvignon is a dry, restrained rosé in the typically French style. Muted aromas lead to bright lemon flavors tinged with wet stones, red currant, raspberry, and a touch of red apple skin. Medium-bodied with 12% alc.

Big House Pink, California, USA

You would never confuse this blend of 10 grape varieties for a White Zinfandel but you might mistake it for a well-made Côtes de Provence rosé with its gentle flavors and aromas of ruby grapefruit, lemon, apple, and stones. It's a delicate and sophisticated mix of fruit and mineral flavors. Full-bodied with 13% alc.

BEST

Folie á Deux Ménage à Trois Rosé Table Wine, California, USA

Shiny fuchsia wine with sweet aromas of strawberry-vanilla and an intense palate of glazed wild cherries and ultra-ripe strawberries. This is an off-dry rosé with balancing acidity and a lick of vanilla cream on the finish. Full-bodied with 13.5% alc.

Some Like It Dry

Softly sweet, accessible pink wines are hugely popular in the United States. Americans drank 41.9 million cases of these wines in 2007 with nearly half attributed to White Zinfandel. If you're looking for a drier, crisper pink wine, look to the Rosés from France, Rosados from Spain, or Rosatos from Italy—or the Big House Pink from California recommended here.

Premium Pink

There's a new estate called Chateau D'Esclans in Provence spinning out very exciting, stylish, and complex $100 bottles of rosé, making them the most expensive pink wines in the world today outside of Champagne.

17

Sparkling Wine

It's easy to think of sparkling wine as alcoholic pop or simply toast tipple. But it's wine. With bubbles. And like all wine, its responsibility is to yield concentration, complexity, and balance. Sure, the style requires it to be lighter than your average still wine but it should always retain the essential hallmarks of a fine wine. Bubbles are secondary.

And like still wine, the best bubblies make polished aperitifs yet can hold their own at the dinner table—the two roles that have never really been shed in Europe, where the style originated. Let's face it; persistent bubbles beading up through a flute lend sparkle to any occasion.

In case you're wondering why the term Champagne isn't used here to describe sparkling wine, it's because Champagne is a wine made in the region of the same name in northern France. The term is sometimes used for sparkling wines made in the style of Champagne, but this copycat labeling bugs the French, who are lobbying the American government for stricter wine labeling laws.

Controversial names notwithstanding, you will find some excellent American "Champagnes" in this chapter that are more affordable than their French counterparts, as well as some stellar Spumante and Asti (Italian sparkling wines), Cava (fizz from Spain), and bubblies from Australia. Drum roll, please ....

Cook's Brut California Champagne, California, USA

This great-value sparkling wine has gentle aromas of green pear and flavors of cool cooked apple. Soft sweetness hovers behind taut fruit and the suggestion of crushed stones. A well-balanced, elegant bubbly. Medium-bodied with 12% alc.

Cook's Spumante California Sparkling Wine, California, USA

This pale and glossy straw-colored fizz brims with attractive aromas of stewed pears and succulent flavors of pears, apples, and peaches poached in sugar. Although it's sweet enough to pair with fresh fruit—or even wedding cake—the refreshing acidity offsets the sugar perfectly. Light-bodied with 8.5% alc.

BEST

Ballatore Gran Spumante California Sparkling Wine, California, USA

This refined, straw-colored wine exudes misty sea-spray aromas before flavors of cooked apple and fresh, ripe pear strike the palate and taper to a baked pear finish. There's some sweetness here but it's well-balanced with razor acidity. Light-bodied with 8% alc.

How Sweet It Is
For sparkling wines, the following terms can appear on labels to indicate increasing levels of sweetness: extra brut (bone dry), brut (dry), extra-dry (off-dry), sec (medium-dry), demi-sec (medium-sweet), doux (sweet), and moelleux (very sweet). Aside from the fact extra-dry is confusingly sweeter than brut, it's all fairly logical if you can remember, with wine, dry is the opposite of sweet. I should also mention that the level of sweetness within each category can vary by producer, so one brand's brut is another brand's sec.

How Many Glasses per Bottle?
One 750 ml bottle of sparkling wine yields about six 4-oz. servings. Pour an average-size flute to the halfway point and you've got a 4-oz. serving.

A Bit of History
The Romans made sparkling wine called spumante as early as the third century B.C.E., well before French Champagne was first produced in the 1700s.

ROSÉ/SPARKLING

[yellow tail] Sparkling Rosé Wine, Australia

This very pale coral-colored sparkler has delicate flavors and aromas of candied citrus and strawberry. Crisp acidity balances the subtle sweetness. Medium-bodied with 12% alc.

[yellow tail] Sparkling White Wine, Australia

This pale straw-colored sparkling wine could easily be mistaken for Prosecco if tasted blind. Think subtle notes of tropical fruit, pear, and nuts on the nose and palate. Off-dry, restrained, and delicate with fresh acidity. Medium-bodied with 12% alc.

BEST

Martini & Rossi Asti Sparkling Wine, Italy

Fresh, vivid flavors and aromas of elderflower cordial, pear, and ripe green grapes imbue this aromatic medium-sweet sparkler. High acidity means it finishes clean and dry. It's certainly an outstanding aperitif yet it's also sweet enough to pair with dessert, including wedding cake. Light-bodied with 7% alc.

Wedding Wine
The biggest travesty occurs when bone-dry bubbly is drunk with wedding cake. Drink dry bubbly with sweets and the wine's tart nature strikes the palate like battery acid. The solution: Serve dry sparkling wine on its own or with savory foods. Then, for a cake-time toast tipple, pour a fairly sweet bubbly, such as Martini & Rossi Asti, or a dessert wine.

ROSÉ/SPARKLING

Freixenet Cordon Negro Brut Cava, Sant Sadurni D'Andia, Spain

This traditional blend of Macabeo, Xarel-lo, and Parellado is dry and very restrained to the point of austerity with dusty apple, white grapefruit, and bread dough notes that finish with a bitter twist. Medium-bodied with 12% alc.

Korbel Brut Rosé California Champagne, California, USA

Unlike French Champagne, this Californian version blends Pinot Noir with Chenin Blanc and French Colombard—instead of Chardonnay and Pinot Meunier—to create a wine with flavors and aromas of red apple, honeydew melon, and strawberry before finishing with a soft note of pink grapefruit. Off-dry and balanced with considerable finesse. Medium-bodied with 12% alc.

For the Record
Freixenet is often
mispronounced. It is
actually pronounced
fresh-eh-NET.

Korbel Brut California Champagne, California, USA

Very attractive aromas of
butter pastry and cooked
apple laced with brown
sugar, nutmeg, and cin-
namon lead to flavors of
homemade apple crumble
and a long, lingering
butter-nut finish. Dry with
racy acidity and impeccable
balance. You would be hard
pressed to find a better
bubbly under $15.
Medium-bodied with
12% alc.

It's a Hit
Korbel is the number one
sparkling wine brand in
the United States with
16 percent of market
share, which is not sur-
prising. It's an incredible
wine for the money
and has spent many
years earning consumer
trust. Korbel Winery was
established in 1882 in
California's Russian River
Valley.

ROSÉ/SPARKLING

Bargain Wines, Dessert Wines, and Party Wines

Good Deals at Super-Low Prices

Ready for a shocker? The best-selling wine in America comes in a box—it's Franzia Winetaps. The second best-selling wine is also seriously inexpensive; it's Carlo Rossi, which comes in those iconic jugs. In fact, 8 of the top 12 best-selling brands cost less than $5 per 750 ml.

For centuries, Europeans have been making and drinking huge quantities of locally-produced, inexpensive wine. Clearly, Americans are doing the same. The only difference is European jug wines tend to be drier and less fruity than their American counterparts. The disparity is not too surprising; Europeans prefer a bit more restraint and dryness in their wine while Americans like a rounder, fruitier style.

Although Americans drink cheap wine most of the time, you seldom see these wines written up in newspaper columns or otherwise assessed by independent critics. So how do you know which bottle to buy when the occasion calls for simplicity itself? Therein lays the purpose of this chapter: To reveal the best wines at super-low prices, complete with tasting notes. All of the wines recommended here cost less than $5 per 750 ml.

Quite frankly, it's shocking just how many wines in this price bracket are pleasures to drink.

Carlo Rossi Rhine, California, USA

Candied lime on the nose leads to an off-dry attack of candied lime, green apple, and ruby grapefruit—with a sassy squeeze of lime-squirt acidity. An easy aperitif. Light-bodied with 9% alc.

Carlo Rossi Chablis, California, USA

Delicate lemon-lime aromas lead to a trim palate of restrained apple and mixed citrus fruits. A very elegant white wine for the price. Crisp and dry with the slightest whisper of sweetness to round out the edges. Light-bodied with 9.5% alc.

Gallo Family Vineyards Twin Valley Moscato, California, USA

This is a downright steal. Exuberant aromas of honeyed peach, lychee, and orange lead to robust flavors of the same. The considerable sweetness is beautifully balanced with palate-cleansing acidity. This would be a great match for fresh fruit at the end of a meal. It would also make a luscious but lively aperitif or Sunday afternoon tipple with butter pound cake. Light-bodied with 9% alc.

Gallo Family Vineyards Twin Valley Merlot, California, USA

Subtle cherry aromas lead to approachable and refreshing black and red cherry flavors. A slight grip on the finish gives it the structure to stand up to a range of foods. Full-bodied with 13% alc.

Gallo Family Vineyards Twin Valley Hearty Burgundy, California, USA

Poached red plums and dark berries on the nose lead to fairly rich, brambly-fruited flavors edged with spicy oak. This well-balanced tipple is a great value. Medium- to full-bodied with 13% alc.

Livingston Cellars Burgundy, California, USA

This light, dry, berry-scented red with an attractive note of dry earthiness subtly recalls its French namesake. Drier than many other wines at this price point, this wine could easily be mistaken for a good quality French jug wine. Light- to medium-bodied with 12% alc.

GOOD

BETTER

Carlo Rossi Reserve Merlot, California, USA

This soft, supple, cherry-scented Merlot has a sweet fruit core, a hint of spice, and a silky mouthfeel. Impressive value. Medium-bodied with 12% alc.

Carlo Rossi Burgundy, California, USA

This round, light, juicy wine is imbued with smooth strawberry and raspberry notes. A good, honest table wine. Light-to medium-bodied with 12% alc.

**Carlo Rossi Reserve
Cabernet Sauvignon,
California, USA**

A clean, well-made, classic
Cabernet Sauvignon at a
bargain price. Pure blackcurrant aromas and flavors
with a round mouthfeel
and a bit of ripe tannic grip
on the finish. Medium-
bodied with 12% alc.

GOOD

BETTER

**Franzia House Wine
Favorites Chillable Red,
California, USA**

Shining the color of
cranberry juice, this wine
exudes aromas of glazed
cherries and medium-sweet
flavors of cranberry, cherry,
and strawberry. Bright and
balanced with nervy acidity,
this makes a great cocktail
alternative or refresher
with spicy fare. Light-
bodied with 9% alc.

**Cellars of Fairbanks
California Port,
California, USA**

For the price, this is not
a bad little red, Port-style
wine. Tastes richly-fruited
with clean flavors of sweet
cherries, blackberries,
Christmas cake, and to-
bacco. It's properly sweet
but very well-balanced.
Full-bodied with 18% alc.

Livingston Cellars Sangria, California, USA

Here's a great red wine alternative. What I love about this Sangria is that it tastes homemade. It brims with flavors of freshly-squeezed oranges and limes with a splash of clean red wine and a nice light spritz. It's more tart than sweet with a hint of bitter lime zest on the finish. Serve it on the rocks with slices of orange and lime. Light-bodied with 10% alc.

BARGAIN, DESSERT, PARTY

Livingston Cellars Blush Chablis, California, USA

Here's a glossy petal-pink wine that starts with some gently floral aromas before striking the palate with crisp but off-dry flavors of peach, strawberry, lavender, and soft rose. Light-bodied with 9% alc.

Gallo Family Vineyards Twin Valley White Zinfandel, California, USA

This great-value quaffer shines a glossy wild salmon color and brims with bright, juicy, softly-sweet flavors of strawberry and white peach. A quenching and light-bodied wine with 9% alc.

BEST

Sutter Home Family Vineyards White Zinfandel, California, USA

This is the best-selling White Zin in America, and it's easy to see why. Gleaming silvery pink in the glass, the peach, orange, cantaloupe, and subtle strawberry flavors are delicate and off-dry with a good edge of incising acidity. Light-bodied with 9.5% alc.

It's a Fact

White Zinfandel was created accidentally at Sutter Home Winery. To increase concentration in the maker's red Zinfandel wines in the 1970s, Sutter Home extracted juice early in the winemaking process and used it to make a dry so-called White Zinfandel. In 1975, a batch of this White Zinfandel stopped fermenting before the yeast had consumed all the sugar, leaving a wine that was light in alcohol and sweet. Tasting it later, the winemaker liked it, bottled it, and tried to sell it. It was a huge hit and the style remains popular today.

BARGAIN,
DESSERT, PARTY

André Peach Passion Sparkling Wine, California, USA

This sweet sparkler tastes of chin-drip peaches with sufficient mouthwatering crispness to refresh sip after sip. It's a delightful cocktail alternative with a light body and less than 11% alc.

Wycliff Brut California Champagne, California, USA

Excellent value for the price. This is a dry—but not bone dry—sparkler with crisp yet restrained flavors and aromas of apple and soft lemon. Light-bodied with 9.5% alc.

André Extra Dry California Champagne, California, USA

Not bad at all! Subtle aromas of peach and pear lead to off-dry, restrained flavors of gala apple and candied citrus peel. This well-made sparkling wine finishes cool, crisp, and dry. Light-bodied with 9.5% alc.

19

Dessert Wine

The best dessert wines are complex, potent, and generally sweet drinks that linger on the palate for ages, recalling such flavors as honeyed peach, dried fruit, roasted nuts, and warm toffee. They punctuate meals perfectly, so it is quite amazing that dessert wines remain an occasional indulgence while having dessert is pretty much a daily occurrence in America. I would rather have a nip of Late Harvest wine than a slice of chocolate cake or apple pie any day.

Although the $$, $$$, and $$$$ price brackets apply here, two more are tacked on—$$$$$ ($15–$19.99) and $$$$$$ ($20–$30)—to account for the fact that many fine dessert wines cost more to make and, therefore, to buy.

Also, this chapter groups wines by bottle price (with sizes noted) rather than cost per volume because these styles often come in 375 ml or 500 ml as well as the usual 750 ml size.

One more thing: in some cases, the recommended dessert wines may not be quite as easy to find as the table wines in this book due to smaller production volumes. That said, the chapter remains focused on popular brands in every price bracket, so your local shop will probably carry at least some of these delicious dessert wines.

Now you have no reason not to indulge.

Sheffield Cellars Oak Mellowed Cream Sherry of California, USA (750 ml)

This pale amber wine is filled with flavors of oranges, caramel, nuts, allspice, and clove. It's a quite complex and classic-tasting sweet Sherry at a remarkably low price. Full-bodied with 18% alc.

Sheffield Cellars Silver Lane Oak Mellowed Marsala of California, USA (750 ml)

Who said Marsala is only for cooking? This pale amber sweetie is rich in flavors and aromas of pralines, butterscotch, dried fig, toasted hazelnut, and a hint of coffee and coconut. Certainly a great choice for your favorite chicken Marsala recipe but also delicious with a handful of dry-roasted nuts or a slice of Parmigiano-Reggiano. Full-bodied with 18% alc.

DESSERT WINES $$

Marsala
Marsala is a fortified wine made in the area surrounding the city of Marsala in Sicily, Italy. It's made from indigenous grape varieties and can be dry or sweet, amber or ruby—but is always warmly alcoholic with levels between 17% and 20%.

Sheffield Cellars Oak Mellowed Very Dry Sherry of California, USA (750 ml)

This pale, dry wine is a terrific value fino-style Sherry with classic yeasty aromas and flavors and a distinct sea salt nuance typical of the style. Although technically a dessert wine, fino Sherry is much better before a meal, served chilled as an aperitif with olives. Full-bodied with 18% alc.

Harveys Bristol Cream, Jerez De La Frontera, Spain (375 ml)

Despite its reputation as being a bit old-fashioned, Harveys Bristol Cream is the world's best-selling Sherry—across all styles. This great by-the-fire drink is an amber-colored, sweet wine with caramelized pecan aromas that lead to bold flavors of roasted nuts, orange oil, raisin, melting toffee, and sweet spices such as nutmeg, cinnamon, and clove. Full-bodied with 17.5% alc.

Dubonnet Rouge Grand Aperitif de France, France (750 ml)

Aromas of sweet cherries and homemade cranberry sauce lead to complex flavors of red cherry, lemon zest, cardamom, red pepper, coffee, almond, and the faintest hint of spearmint before tapering to a long orange oil finish. You'll love the smooth and polished mouthfeel. Full-bodied with 14.8% alc.

BEST

Warre's Warrior Reserve Port, Douro, Portugal (375 ml)

This dark red port exudes a rich perfume of stewed berries and plums before striking the palate with flavors of black cherry, dried fig, plum pudding, milk chocolate, mixed spices, and creamy vanilla. Velvety, intense, and sweet with a long, warm, smoked cinnamon finish. Definitely one for the cheeseboard. Full-bodied with 20% alc.

Food Pairing
Harveys Bristol Cream is best served with aged Gouda, sipped with a handful of roasted nuts, or drizzled over maple walnut ice cream.

Serving It Right
Most dessert wines recommended in this chapter are best served slightly chilled, so take them out of the refrigerator 20 minutes before serving. The only exception is Dubonnet, which is best served on the rocks with a good squeeze of lemon.

BARGAIN,
DESSERT, PARTY

Pellegrino Moscato di Pantelleria, Sicily, Italy (375 ml)

This pale golden wine starts with pronounced aromas of roses and almonds then offers rich flavors of honeyed grapes, roses, honeysuckle, and a long, warm almond finish. Sweet yet crisp. Full-bodied with 15% alc.

Dow's Late Bottled Vintage Port, Douro, Portugal (375 ml)

This excellent value Late Bottled Vintage (LBV) starts with powerful aromas of cassis and mixed berries before striking the palate with intense black and red fruit, peppercorn, smoke, and wood. Although sweet, it's drier than most other LBV Ports with a tight tannic grip. A long, intense, serious wine with a dry finish. Full-bodied with 20% alc.

BEST

**Graham's Six Grapes Reserve
Port, Douro, Portugal
(375 ml)**

Like LBV, this Port is
made to taste similar to
Vintage Port without the
fuss of decanting or further
aging. It starts with intense
cherry-almond and anise
aromas that give way to
flavors of cherry, sweet
tobacco, almonds, anise,
blackberry, coffee, cream,
milk chocolate, and vanilla.
Incredibly well-made and
complex. This is a seriously
underpriced wine. Full-
bodied with 20% alc.

LBV vs. Vintage
Although Late Bottled
Vintage tastes similar
to the more premium
Vintage Port, there are
three big differences
between the two styles.
LBV is bottled ready to
drink while Vintage Port
requires decades in bottle
to reach maturity. Vintage
Port needs to be decanted
to separate it from its
sediment while LBV does
not. And, although LBV is
not as rich and decadent
as a mature Vintage Port, it
is far more affordable.

**Sugar Adds Weight
to Wine**
Although wines with
lower alcohol levels are
generally light in body,
sweet wines can be an
exception. Since sugar
also adds weight to wine,
you often find full-bodied
dessert wines such as Late
Harvests with surprisingly
low alcohol levels of 12%
or less.

Concha y Toro Late Harvest Sauvignon Blanc, Maule Valley, Maipo, Chile (375 ml)

This straw-colored wine tastes of lime marmalade, honey, mango, and pear. It's a lively and aromatic dessert wine that's lusciously sweet with balancing acidity. The high sugar content gives it significant weight in the mouth, making it quite full-bodied despite only 12% alc.

Pellegrino Passito di Pantelleria DOC, Sicily, Italy (375 ml)

Subtle orange oil aromas lead to pronounced flavors of orange peel, dried apricots, and peach conserve before finishing with a lingering apricot aftertaste and a final note of orange zest. Succulent and balanced, this wine is the ideal accompaniment to almond cookies such as biscotti. Full-bodied with 15% alc.

DESSERT WINES $$$$$

BEST

Kendall-Jackson Late Harvest Chardonnay, Jackson Estates Grown, Monterey, California (375 ml)

This deep golden wine starts with aromas of honey and orange marmalade then leads to fresh yet luscious flavors of the same, layered with apple, kiwi, and stewed peach with a bright fresh orange tang on the finish. Incredibly delicious and hugely undervalued. It tastes very sweet but finishes clean and dry. Full-bodied because of the high sugar yet only 11% alc.

Noble Rot
The grapes in Kendall-Jackson Late Harvest Chardonnay and Concha y Toro Late Harvest Sauvignon Blanc were infected with "Noble Rot," known technically as Botrytis. This benevolent form of a grey fungus coats the grapes and shrivels them on the vine, concentrating the sugars and imparting a telltale marmalade character to the final wine.

Passito Is ...
An Italian term for dried grape wine. Passito winemaking involves drying grapes after they're picked to concentrate their sugars before fermentation, which results in a sweet wine.

How Long Will Port and Sherry Keep?
Once opened, aged Tawny Port and sweeter styles of Sherry will keep for up to four months in the refrigerator. Ruby, Reserve, and LBV Port will keep for three weeks if kept cold. Vintage Port does not keep well once opened and decanted.

BARGAIN, DESSERT, PARTY

GOOD

Warre's Otima 10 Year Old Tawny Port, Douro, Portugal (500 ml)

This Tawny packaged with a modern look is all about walnuts and toffee with hints of dried currants and a long nutmeg, clove, white pepper, and cinnamon finish. It's quite sweet but well-balanced. Full-bodied with 20% alc.

BETTER

Graham's Tawny Port Aged 20 Years, Douro, Portugal (375 ml)

This very refined Tawny offers aromas and flavors of Brazil nut, orange peel, dried fig, raisin, toffee, and fruitcake. It's smooth, sweet, and balanced with a long finish reminiscent of ground Brazil nuts. Full-bodied with 20% alc.

$$$$$$

BEST

Taylor Fladgate 10 Year Old Tawny Port, Douro, Portugal (750 ml)

Aged for 10 years in wood, this stellar Tawny is just gorgeous. It starts with almond and caramel aromas with some subtle cherry charm. Then, on the palate, comes a vibrant rush of flavor—all the glorious, warm, walnut-toffee-orange-fig complexity of an old Tawny but shot through with vivacious red fruits. Simply delicious and miles ahead of the pack. Full-bodied with 20% alc.

BARGAIN, DESSERT, PARTY

20

Party Wine

When it's party time, wine becomes so much more than a drink. It becomes a social lubricant, a point of communion, and a topic of discussion. It also displays rather conspicuously the host's personal taste, level of sophistication, and budget. No wonder the selection process can be daunting.

Yet pouring a simple or inexpensive wine isn't always blush-worthy; if it's undervalued, delicious, stylishly presented, and seasonally appropriate, the choice is flattering. For instance, a well-made $6 White Zinfandel is the perfect pour at an outdoor wedding reception on the lake. But the same wine would look awkwardly out of place at, say, a private dinner party for six with a perfectly roasted bird or prime rib. The latter occasion calls for something more distinguished like a stunning Pinot Noir or wooded Chardonnay.

That's where this chapter comes in. It presents the good, better, and best wines for every style of party, taking into account mood, setting, and decorum. Every wine recommended has broad general appeal, is unquestionably appropriate, and is seriously underpriced. So without further ado …

WEDDING RECEPTION

WHITES

Folonari Soave DOC, Veneto, Italy ($$)

(see pg. 28)

Citra Pinot Grigio IGT, Sicily, Italy ($$)

(see pg. 51)

Mirassou Pinot Grigio, California, USA ($$$$)

(see pg. 55)

REDS

Big House Red, California, USA ($$)

(see pg. 91)

Citra Montepulciano d'Abruzzo DOC, Abruzzo, Italy ($$)

(see pg. 166)

Columbia Crest Two Vines Cabernet Sauvignon, Washington State, USA ($$$)

(see pg. 107)

GOOD

BETTER

BEST

Wine Selection Criteria

Wedding reception wines should have a classic air about them. They should be agreeable enough to appeal to all guests without tasting dull or boring. And they should pair easily with food, be widely available, and reasonably-priced. Tick all these boxes and you're on track.

WEDDING RECEPTION

ROSÉS

Sutter Home Family Vineyards White Zinfandel, California, USA ($)

(see pg. 207)

Barefoot White Zinfandel, California, USA ($$)

(see pg. 182)

Beringer California Collection White Zinfandel, California, USA ($$)

(see pg. 183)

SPARKLING WINES

Ballatore Gran Spumante California Sparkling Wine, California, USA ($$)

(see pg. 189)

Korbel Brut California Champagne, California, USA ($$$$)

(see pg. 193)

Martini & Rossi Asti Sparkling Wine, Italy ($$$)

(see pg. 191)

WEDDING RECEPTION

SWEET WINES

GOOD

Pellegrino Moscato di Pantelleria, Sicily, Italy (375 ml)($$$$)

(see pg. 216)

BETTER

Sutter Home Family Vineyards Moscato, California, USA ($$)

(see pg. 77)

BEST

Barefoot Cellars "Deliciously Sweet" Moscato, California, USA ($$)

(see pg. 79)

DINNER PARTY

WHITES

Kendall-Jackson Vintner's Reserve Riesling, California, USA ($$$$)

(see pg. 73)

Robert Mondavi Winery Fumé Blanc, Napa Valley, California, USA ($$$$)

(see pg. 65)

Sterling Vintner's Collection Chardonnay, Central Coast, California, USA ($$$)

(see pg. 41)

REDS

Columbia Crest Grand Estates Shiraz, Washington State, USA ($$$$)

(see pg. 143)

Bogle Vineyards Pinot Noir, Russian River Valley, California, USA ($$$$)

(see pg. 155)

Rodney Strong Sonoma County Cabernet Sauvignon, California, USA ($$$$)

(see pg. 109)

Wine Selection Criteria
Dinner party wines should be complex, elegant, refined concoctions that enhance the food but not overpower it. Labels should be attractive since the bottles grace the tables. And selecting a wine by a reputable producer suggests you know your stuff.

BARGAIN, DESSERT, PARTY

DINNER PARTY

SPARKLING WINES

DESSERT WINES

GOOD

Freixenet Cordon Negro Brut Cava, Sant Sadurni D'Andia, Spain ($$$$)

(see pg. 192)

Taylor Fladgate 10 Year Old Tawny Port, Douro, Portugal (750 ml)($$$$$$)

(see pg. 221)

BETTER

Korbel Brut Rosé California Champagne, California, USA ($$$$)

(see pg. 192)

Pellegrino Passito di Pantelleria DOC, Sicily, Italy (375 ml) ($$$$$)

(see pg. 218)

BEST

Korbel Brut California Champagne, California, USA ($$$$)

(see pg. 193)

Kendall-Jackson Late Harvest Chardonnay, Jackson Estates Grown, Monterey, California (375 ml) ($$$$$)

(see pg. 219)

Etiquette Tip
Must the host or hostess open the wine a guest brings to a dinner party? Absolutely not. And yes, it's usually rude for the guest to suggest it.

COCKTAIL PARTY

WHITES

Relax Riesling, Mosel, Germany ($$$)

(see pg. 70)

Kim Crawford Marlborough Sauvignon Blanc, Marlborough, New Zealand ($$$$)

(see pg. 64)

Cavit Collection Pinot Grigio Delle Venezie IGT, Italy ($$$)

(see pg. 53)

REDS

Trapiche Varietals Malbec, Mendoza, Argentina ($$)

(see pg. 167)

Big House "The Lineup" GSM Red Wine, Central Coast, California ($$$$)

(see pg. 97)

Concha y Toro Casillero del Diablo Syrah, Rapel Valley, Chile ($$$$)

(see pg. 145)

Wine Selection Criteria
At cocktail parties, the wines should be of a high standard and made from well-known grape varieties to put guests at ease. Ideal "cocktail" wines are rich in fruit, beautifully balanced and a little complex.

COCKTAIL PARTY

ROSÉS SPARKLING WINES

GOOD

Barefoot White Zinfandel, California, USA ($$)

(see pg. 182)

André Extra Dry California Champagne, California, USA ($)

(see pg. 209)

BETTER

Beringer California Collection White Zinfandel, California, USA ($$)

(see pg. 183)

Ballatore Gran Spumante California Sparkling Wine, California, USA ($$)

(see pg. 189)

BEST

Folie à Deux Ménage à Trois Rosé Table Wine, California, USA ($$$)

(see pg. 185)

Korbel Brut Rosé California Champagne, California, USA ($$$$)

(see pg. 192)

BACKYARD BARBECUE

WHITES	REDS

Trapiche Broquel Torrontés, Mendoza, Argentina ($$$$)

(see pg. 82)

Bogle Vineyards Petite Sirah, California, USA ($$$)

(see pg. 169)

Dancing Bull Sauvignon Blanc, California, USA ($$$$)

(see pg. 63)

Sebeka Shiraz Pinotage "Cape Blend," Western Cape, South Africa

(see pg. 93)

Starborough Marlborough Sauvignon Blanc, Marlborough, New Zealand ($$$$)

(see pg. 62)

Dancing Bull Zinfandel, California, USA ($$$$)

(see pg. 163)

Wine Selection Criteria

The backyard barbecue requires full-fruited wines that stand up to the charred flavors of grilled foods. And, since barbecues are held in warm weather, the wines need bright acidity to keep guests feeling refreshed after each sip.

BACKYARD BARBECUE

GOOD

Beringer California Collection White Zinfandel, California, USA ($$)

(see pg. 183)

BETTER

Folie à Deux Ménage à Trois Rosé Table Wine, California, USA ($$$)

(see pg. 185)

BEST

Barefoot White Zinfandel, California, USA ($$)

(see pg. 182)

BEACH/POOL/COTTAGE PARTY

WHITES	REDS

 **Fünf 5 German Riesling, Germany ($$)**

(see pg. 69)

 **Livingston Cellars Burgundy, California, USA ($)**

(see pg. 201)

 **Riunite Bianco, Italy ($$)**

(see pg. 29)

 **Riunite Lambrusco IGT, Emilia, Italy ($$$)**

(see pg. 170)

 Carlo Rossi Chablis, California, USA ($)

(see pg. 198)

 **Livingston Cellars Sangria, California, USA ($)**

(see pg. 201)

Wine Selection Criteria
For these quintessentially casual affairs, choose cheap and cheerful favorites, venture into the world of alternative packaging like boxes and plastic, always include some light and quenching choices, and let the good times roll.

BARGAIN, DESSERT, PARTY

BEACH/COTTAGE/POOL PARTY

ROSÉS

Livingston Cellars Blush Chablis, California, USA ($)

(see pg. 206)

Gallo Family Vineyards Twin Valley White Zinfandel, California, USA ($)

(see pg. 206)

Sutter Home Family Vineyards White Zinfandel, California, USA in four-packs of 187 ml unbreakable plastic bottles ($$)

(see pg. 207)

GOOD

BETTER

BEST

Beware

If you plan to serve boxed wine, tread carefully. A lot of it is still terribly confected and thin. This book reveals some of the better choices in the category.

GARDEN PARTY

WHITES

Santa Margherita Pinot Grigio, Alto Adige DOC, Italy ($$$$ for a half bottle)

Refreshing, delicate, and complex.

Loredona Viognier, Lodi, California, USA ($$$$)

(see pg. 83)

Chateau Ste. Michelle Dry Riesling, Columbia Valley, Washington State, USA ($$$$)

(see pg. 72)

REDS

Cavit Collection Pinot Noir, Provincia di Pavia IGT, Italy ($$$)

(see pg. 150)

J. Lohr Estates Wildflower Valdiguié, Monterey County, California, USA ($$$)

(see pg. 171)

Mark West Pinot Noir, Sonoma County, California, USA ($$$)

(see pg. 151)

Wine Selection Criteria
Garden parties hail from Britain and have a whiff of frilly formality to them. The wines therefore should be crisp, refreshing, and of a high standard. And never forget the Late Harvest or Moscato with juicy peaches for dessert!

GARDEN PARTY

	ROSÉS	SPARKLING WINES

GOOD

Sutter Home Family Vineyards White Zinfandel, California, USA ($)

(see pg. 207)

Martini & Rossi Asti Sparkling Wine, Italy ($$$)

(see pg. 191)

BETTER

Le Rosé de Mouton Cadet, Baron Philippe de Rothschild, Bordeaux Rosé AC, Bordeaux, France ($$$)

(see pg. 184)

Korbel Brut Rosé California Champagne, California, USA

(see pg. 192)

BEST

Big House Pink, California, USA ($$$)

(see pg. 184)

Korbel Brut California Champagne, California, USA ($$$$)

(see pg. 193)

How Much Wine?

The standard amount of wine to plan for a party is ½ a bottle per person if wine is the main beverage. One extra bottle for every five guests is also a good idea.

GARDEN PARTY

**Concha y Toro
Late Harvest
Sauvignon
Blanc, Maule
Valley, Maipo,
Chile (375 ml)
($$$$$)**

(see pg. 218)

**Kendall-Jackson
Late Harvest
Chardonnay,
Jackson Es-
tates Grown,
Monterey, Cali-
fornia (375 ml)
($$$$$)**

(see pg. 219)

**Sutter Home
Family
Vineyards
Moscato,
California, USA
($$)**

(see pg. 77)

BANQUETS

WHITES	REDS

GOOD

Trapiche Varietals Torrontés, Mendoza, Argentina ($$)

(see pg. 78)

Woodbridge by Robert Mondavi Cabernet Sauvignon, California, USA ($$)

(see pg. 102)

BETTER

Folonari Soave DOC, Veneto, Italy ($$)

(see pg. 28)

Bella Sera Pinot Noir, Provincia di Pavia, Italy ($$)

(see pg. 148)

BEST

Citra Pinot Grigio IGT, Sicily, Italy ($$)

(see pg. 51)

Citra Montepulciano d'Abruzzo DOC, Abruzzo, Italy ($$)

(see pg. 166)

Wine Selection Criteria
These occasions call for food-friendly choices that are both classic and inexpensive but neither dull nor deadly cheap. And all that's required is a red and a white.